Blonde Indian

VOLUME 57

Sun Tracks

An American Indian Literary Series

Blonde Indian

AN ALASKA NATIVE MEMOIR

Ernestine Hayes

The University of Arizona Press   TUCSON

The University of Arizona Press

© 2006 Ernestine Hayes

⊗ This book is printed on acid-free, archival-quality paper.

Manufactured in the United States of America

11 10 09 08 07 06   6 5 4 3 2 1

Library of Congress Cataloging-in-Publication Data

Hayes, Ernestine, 1945–

Blonde Indian : an Alaska Native memoir / Ernestine Hayes.

p. cm. — (Sun tracks ; v. 57)

IBSN-13: 978-0-8165-2538-6 (hardcover : alk. paper)

IBSN-10: 0-8165-2538-2 (hardcover : alk. paper)

IBSN-13: 978-0-8165-2537-9 (pbk. : alk. paper)

IBSN-10: 0-8165-2537-4 (pbk. : alk. paper)

1. Hayes, Ernestine, 1945– 2. Tlingit Indians—Alaska—
Biography. 3. Tlingit women—Alaska—Biography. 4. Tlingit
Indians—Alaska—Social life and customs. 5. Alaska—Social
life and customs. I. Title. II. Series.

PS501.S85 vol. 57

[E99]

979.8004′97270092—dc22   2005037307

Publication of this book is made possible in part by the
proceeds of a permanent endowment created with the assistance
of a Challenge Grant from the National Endowment for the
Humanities, a federal agency.

To the memory of my mother and the promise of my sons

CONTENTS

One of my first jobs after I came back home to Juneau was at a Native theater, where we told old stories and sang and drummed old songs. At the
end of each performance, we stood in a line on the stage and introduced
ourselves in our Native language, and then translated what we had just
said. I would say: *Lingít x'eináx Saankaláxt' yóo xat du waa sáak'w*: My Tlingit
name is Saankaláxt. *Dleit káa x'eináx* Ernestine Hayes *yóo xat du waa sáak'w*:
My white man name is Ernestine Hayes. *Ch'aak' naa ayá xát*: I am Eagle.
Kaagwaantaan ayá xát: I am of the Burnt House People Clan. *Gooch hít ayá
xát*: I belong to the Wolf House. *Gunáx teidí dach xan xát sitée*: I am a grandchild of the Gunaxteidi. *Yan wa sháa*: I am a Kaagwaantaan woman. *Sheet'ká
Kwáan*: My clan springs from Sitka.

The woman standing next to me would step forward and say *Lingít x'einax
Kaastéen yóo xat du waa sáak'w. Chookaneidí ayá xát*: I am of the people from
the grassy place, and I belong to Glacier Bay.

And I loved to hear her say that, for it describes our relationship to the
land. Who our land now belongs to, or if land can even be owned, is a question for politicians and philosophers. But we belong to the land. There is
not one Lingít person, from the most modern corporate executive to the
most unsophisticated villager, from the oldest great-grandparent whose
dim eyes can see only memories to the youngest child who has just learned
to form the words, who will not say, "This is our land, for we still belong
to it. We belong to Lingít Aaní."

We can't help but place our love there.

Blonde Indian

The Retreating Glacier

Late on a dark night, above the whispers and settlings of the cedar and the spruce, you might hear a woman wailing. Follow that sound into the forest. Take off all your clothes. You will wander a long time as you listen to the woman's grief stir the compassionate trees. After a while you might find her. You will see that she, too, is naked. She is holding a baby and wailing. Why is this woman crying? Maybe her husband has left her. Maybe she wishes he would. Why is she crying? Maybe she has realized that this precious baby will grow away from her, will go away, will cause her pain, will one day die, and so will she. Maybe her grief is for the world.

Now that you have found her, boldly approach and with an irresistible gesture grab the baby from her arms. Now she has something to cry about. Her first grief is forgotten. She will beg you to give her back that baby. Be like a rock against her begging, sternly ignore her whimpers, be very strong. Soon she will offer you promises, and that's when you can have anything you ask. She will give you any gift.

When I was a girl growing up in the village, my grandmother taught me songs. *Blonde Indian, Blonde Indian,* she sang, while I danced and sang and shook my hands. *Blonde Indian, Blonde Indian.* I had light-colored hair when I was a girl. She told me about the spiders that lived in our barewood house, that they were friends who carried stories, and if I listened carefully, I would know what my friends had come to tell me. An only child, I had few other friends. She told me about the Taku Wind howling over our heads on dark winter days, that it was my grandfather letting me know I couldn't come outside and play on those days when he sang his song too loud.

My other grandfather, the one whose white man name I carried, was gone for long months at a time, fishing. When he came back, he made biscuits, holding the baking sheet over his head before dropping it loudly onto the floor and sliding it into the oven of our wood-burning stove. He brought butter to melt on our biscuits, a rare treat—fresh baked biscuits and melted yellow butter.

When we sat at the table to spread butter on our biscuits, my grandmother talked to me about my cousin, the brown bear. She taught me that when I wandered too close to the edge of the forest, picking berries into the Hills Brothers coffee can she hung around my neck by a thin dirty string, I was to talk to my unseen cousin. *Don't bother me, cousin! I'm only here for my share! I'm not trying to bother you!*

Be kind to me, cousin!

She taught me to dig fast for clams on the rich beach, watch for their squirting spit, run fast, dig fast, place my treasured clams carefully into a pail, fill the pail and carry it home, wet hungry beach sand sucking my untied shoes. Scrub the uncomplaining shells in fresh cold water. Watch her cook the sea-flavored clams. Drink the juice. If there is still butter left over from grandfather's last visit, melt a little butter into the broth. Otherwise, maybe some seal oil. Eat the clams with seaweed and salmon eggs. Chew on some dryfish. Drink some Hudson Bay tea. Then, fresh berries I may have picked that very day, berries that my cousin the brown bear had so kindly allowed me to take from the edge of the forest, from where he quietly watched.

Grandmother taught me that all our relatives and friends, even the forest, can hear every word that we say. That is why we must always be careful with our words, she said. Always show respect. Remember who you are. Watch your words carefully. Even the forest can hear you.

Even the forest can hear.

My mother was diagnosed with tuberculosis not long after I was born. For the first few years she was an intermittent patient at the Public Health Hospital across the creek from our old house. Every few days, my grandmother walked me through a field of wildflowers and dewdrops to a window in my mother's quarantine world. My mother and her companions —other tubercular Native women and their nurses—wore white half-masks tied to their faces. They peeked through the window and laughed, their faces framing my mother's hidden smile. Above the masks their eyes squinted laughter; beneath the masks their smiles sparkled through the cotton as they waved. I played in the light rain around the corner from the shady morning side of the building while my grandmother and mother talked. When it was time to go, I said goodbye and watched my mother act out the mask-covered words— "I!" — "love!" — "you!" And I waved and smiled back before we left.

"When you're picking berries," Grandmother said, "always make noise. That way the bear will go away before you see him." She went about her chores, guiding clothes through the wringer washer, stirring stews of fish or deer meat bubbling on the stove. She showed me how to pick out delicate parts of the fish head, how to peel half-formed salmonberry shoots for a tender new taste of green, how to talk to my cousin the brown bear. "If he comes up to you, don't run. Talk to him. Remind him that you're his cousin. Tell him you only want enough berries for you and your family. Tell him you only want your share."

Brown bears and people have often intermarried, hence we are cousins.

We must never eat brown-bear meat; for us, it would be like eating a person. We must always show respect, even when we kill them. Other things should never be killed at all. "You should never kill spiders. They're good luck. They protect you. They tell you secrets," she instructed. "Never kill a spider. It's lucky when they live in your house."

Bears were my cousins and the wind was my grandfather. I had no sisters or brothers and I had few friends, but wild plants grew on the hill beside our old house, and a creek led up the mountain behind me, and seaweed and crabs danced in the ocean channel at my feet. I never questioned that I belonged.

Blonde Indian, Grandmother sang and sometimes danced with me while I dipped my head and shook my hands. *Blonde Indian*. When you don't act right, she said, people will laugh at you. Never forget who you are. Sometimes she took me into South Franklin Street bars and passed me from lap to lap. I showed off by counting in Tlingit and dancing. *Tléix' — Déix — Nás'k — Daax'oon*. Men and women who smelled like Tokay gave me wet winey kisses and handfuls of change. Everyone laughed.

Blonde Indian, Grandmother sang. Listen to our story, the spiders thoughtfully whispered. Don't come too close, my bear cousin fondly warned.

In summer, we boarded a slow ferry to travel with lapping waves around and through the islands of Southeast Alaska, where our people had lived for generations, to a cannery in Hawk Inlet, where my grandmother worked, sliming fish. A row of one-room houses lined a wooden walkway; Native women, heads covered with wrapped scarves tied in flower-decorated knots at the tops of their shiny foreheads, called to one another, sweeping wooden stoops and stopping to tease and flirt and gossip. Smokehouses balanced along the beach added a delicate hint of alder to the salt water air and southeast breeze. Late in the summer we traveled back to our house at the edge of the village in Juneau, where my grandfather readied himself for fall fishing, preparing to be absent until at least the beginning of winter. He would return late in the year, pulling from his pocket a yellow plastic rabbit wearing funny eyeglasses and blue britches, giving me a new bunny trinket each year to add to my collection of wonderful things not to be found in Juneau.

For the remainder of the winter, Uncle Buzz and Uncle Skip ran in and out of the old damp house, raising their voices, grabbing leftover stew or pilot bread and disappearing again, sometimes for days. Aunt Ida lingered behind her bedroom door until evening, when she appeared with a strong smell of sweet perfume, looking like a cotton-candy dream in a bright red jacket of rayon fluff that shed puff trails into the air and onto the wooden floor all the way to the plain front door, where my other grandfather, the Taku Wind, warned us to stay inside.

The hill behind our old house at the edge of the village was my comfortable retreat in the summer; in winter, the floor under the table hid me from my uncles' commotion, from my grandmother and grandfather's noisy arguments, from visitors' overwrought pinches on my sturdy cheeks. When my grandmother enrolled me in school, I was forced to dig around under the cot in the unlit closet where I slept, rummaging for a skirt or underpants or a shirt. Unwashed, I made my way out of Village Street onto the paved sidewalk, around a wide corner and halfway up the hill to a basement room that housed stiffly folded chairs, a basement room where dainty little girls and clean little boys stared at me when I entered, always dirty, always hungry, always late.

Grandma was a slender woman who wore her long silver and steel colored hair wrapped at the back of her head. During the winter, when my grandfather was home for the longest period of time, she powdered her face and drew careful eyebrows in arching lines above her snappy dark eyes. During our Hawk Inlet summers, she spent long days in the cannery while I explored bear trails and nibbled on salmonberries or waded on the beach, investigating tide pools where I imagined new worlds and made pets of trapped minnows.

My mother became a disembodied memory, a signature on regular letters, a scowling/smiling face on infrequent photos, a name in a story my grandmother occasionally told. After my mother was sent by her doctors north to a hospital in Seward, Aunt Ida kept communication open and constant through the mail, letters and black-and-white photos unfailingly supplied to my recuperating mother, now missing half a lung. In photos sent by return mail, my mother brushes her thick, raven-colored wavy hair while she sits on top of a tucked-in hospital bed, her face now metal framed but still smiling through the window of the photo. Her perpetual frown forms a scowl suggesting not anger but fierce courage. In the snapshot of my imagination she shows off to her fellow patients and hospital staff the latest funny picture of her growing baby girl as I pose my way through the years. In my imagination, her loving smile and proud scowl are finally and always unmasked.

My mother stowed those old photos buried in a closet in an unpacked box until years later, back home in Juneau at last, she handed them to me with no explanation. Pictures show a little girl clowning for the camera, as in my memory in earlier years I had clowned for my mother in front of the window on the afternoon side of the government hospital near the village, around the corner from the shady morning side where a tubular slide propelled itself out of a door on the second floor, down which I imagined myself sliding but never would.

I moved back and forth between my grandmother's house in the village and my Aunt Erm's house across the channel, on the beach side of the road to Douglas, a mile or so from the bridge. Aunt Erm grew a garden, and she cooked in the kitchen of Saint Ann's, the hospital for white people to which, in a few years, my then-cured hardworking mother would take her eight-year-old only child to be treated for rheumatic fever, an infection of the heart that eventually leaves lifelong scars on the unsuspecting, untried beating muscle.

Aunt Erm's garden was a wonder of chives and carrots, turnips and spinach, strawberries, nasturtiums, and radishes, everything to be eaten or smelled or pulled from the soft, damp, cool, clinging, good-smelling earth, wiped on the side of a little girl's yellow-fringed fourth-of-july cowboy skirt, bitten and tasted and years later richly remembered. Aunt Erm and her white man husband, Uncle George, kept chickens and rabbits that scurried and clucked and ended up crisp and steaming in bowls filled with buttered noodles and parsley on the Sunday dinner table, along with exotic other foods like gravy and cake that Aunt Erm cooked at her job in the white people's kitchen at the hospital.

In my grandmother's house back across the channel, we ate deer meat and porcupine my uncles poached from land that once belonged to our powerful ancestors, the Kaagwaantaan. We were a warrior clan, but the land was no longer ours. If we wanted deer meat, my uncles had to sneak the deer's carcass to the edge of the trees near the road and wheel me in a wagon in the dark evening, innocently perched on a pile of burlap to cover the deer. When we wanted to boil soup bones, my grandmother sent me to ask for meat scraps from the market. We cut and fried halibut cheeks from the fish heads covering the dock near the cold storage where my grandmother and grandfather sometimes found work sliming fish. Salmon heads for boiling came from the same place. My favorite part was always the softly gristled nose separated by a delicate simmer from the wide-eyed gaping head picked from the cold storage docks. It was past these docks that I sometimes walked on my way to the white people's school.

In first grade, when the chore was learning to read, the lady teacher organized the class into three groups according to reading proficiency. The lowest were Seagulls. Bluebirds were the highest. The girls in the Bluebirds were freckled and clean. I worried that I would have to grow freckles and wear pastel angora sweaters before I could become a Bluebird. I feared I would never be good enough.

Dick, Jane, and Spot live in an oversized, brightly shuttered house with Mother, a yellow-haired woman with white skin and smiling red lips who waves a morning goodbye across the manicured lawn to Father, dressed in a business suit and stepping into a shiny new car. On the next page, Mother dawdles in the kitchen and hums while she bakes chocolate chip cookies and a fine roasted beef. Dick and Jane and Spot frolic with a bright red ball in the sunny yard. Spot is a small, mostly white, frisky dog with a black spot around his right eye. It is a clever, playful name. Dick neatly tucks his striped, colorful shirt into belted trousers. I sense that Jane is a Bluebird.

We laid our heads on our desks and listened to classical music every Monday. On Thursdays we learned about art. On Fridays we sat quietly and listened to Mrs. Green read fairy tales and other fables designed to convey life's truths, most of which I didn't understand but only accepted.

Castles and rosebushes were as foreign to me as my classmates' angora sweaters.

My favorite story to ponder was *The Princess and the Pea*. What is the nature of a princess, I wondered later in life, that something so ambiguous can define you? What makes a woman so precious, so unusual, that she can confidently complain of a trifle, demand and receive such extraordinary favor? Even at my Seagull beginning, I knew I could never balance myself on a pile of twenty mattresses. And I had already learned the stern lesson from my grandmother that a well-born Kaagwaantaan will not complain.

When I walked to school one cloudy morning, the dirt street where in the evenings I played kick the can with other village children was dotted with puddles. Plain, unpainted old houses faced one another along the way; here and there a rack of deerskin leaned against the steps to someone else's uninviting front door. At the end of Village Street I could climb stairs up a steep, berry-filled hill, which would let me turn around at the top of the stairs for a look down at the village. Or I could climb other stairs that began farther up Willoughby Street behind rattletrap apartments and past Native and Filipino houses perched here and there along the hillside. Or I could walk all the way around a wide corner on the paved street and not climb stairs at all. I could walk almost all the way to the cold storage docks past men in yellow rubber suits cutting fish and throwing unwanted fish parts onto the wooden docks where I was often sent to collect the heads for that night's boiled soup. Big men balanced on slimy tables threw cuts of halibut into bins and onto the floor. They shouted and cursed, never looking at one another. Never looking at the little girl sent by her grandma to collect the evening meal.

If I walked past the cold storage on my way to first grade, my path circled the corner gas station, where I could step hard on a dull-red tube stretched across the cement and listen for a bell. White men in greasy blue coveralls glanced without interest as I readied myself to flee, having been warned by my friend Paul that I would be arrested if I stepped on the cord hard enough to make a noise. Going this way would take me halfway back up the hill to the basement room where I attended makeshift school, learning to read.

I walked the long way, skipping past Thibodeau's Market, not open yet.

Even if it were open, I couldn't go in without money in my hand. The people in the market always watched their customers, staring and moving up and down the aisles for a better view. Running past the old apartments, I saw a friend from first grade. "Wait up!" Paul called. "Look what I got!" Paul lived in the pale-green apartments at the foot of the stairs. His black hair was cut short and stood straight up on his head. I had never been invited into his home, but I had often heard noises from inside. Paul's father and mother lived at home, and they yelled a lot. My grandma almost never yelled except when my grandfather was home from fishing and they drank too much Tokay wine. Then they both yelled and got mad and threw chairs. But most of the time my grandfather was gone and our house was quiet.

Paul's outstretched hand held a salmonberry, green and hard. He popped it into his mouth. "Those aren't good yet," I pronounced. "You're not supposed to eat them 'til they're soft. They're not good like that." He dug in his pocket and pulled out another handful of green berries. I chose the brightest one and sucked on it as we walked.

We looked inside Stevenson's Market, halfway up the street. Mr. Stevenson had once given me half of a heavy, thick-skinned ball he said was called a cantaloupe. You have to eat it with a spoon, he told me. The soft orange flesh was a juicy surprise. When I had eaten all of the orange flesh, I scraped the green rind with my teeth until the coarsely lined skin was all that was left. I chewed the dry-tasting skin into an unpleasant pulp and buried the whole wad in shady dirt at the side of our old house, hoping it would grow like the plants in Aunt Erm's garden.

This morning Mr. Stevenson was busy helping a customer, a man we'd seen walking down the street carrying an umbrella over his head. "Do you know what that's called?" Paul whispered, still sucking on sour green salmonberries. "That's called an umbrella. White men use that to walk down the street with. They don't like to get wet when it rains." We looked at the spiky round contraption dripping on the market floor. It swayed and wanted to roll. I stepped close to the counter so I could look at the pictures under the glass. A fat-faced white man smiled up from a poster. I Like Ike, I read.

Crabapple trees grew at the top of a steep, rocky hill next door to the store. Although we'd never seen her, we knew that a mean old lady would run out and shoot us with a BB gun if she caught us picking her apples. We climbed quietly up the muddy hill just enough to get a look at the nearest tree. "They're not ready yet," Paul whispered. "It's still all flowers. They're not even apples yet."

We half-slid down the wet trail. I slipped on a patch of grass and fell face-first onto a pipe sticking up from the wet ground, hitting it with my forehead. For a moment I watched bright light and darkness take turns blinking behind my closed eyes.

Paul ran. I covered one eye with a mud-stained hand. Blood ran down my wrist, down my arm, down my elbow onto the ground. Holding my face, I walked around the corner and halfway up the hill to the basement classroom where first grade was held that year. Children sat in their chairs ready to read.

Every day Mrs. Green separated the children into Seagulls, Wrens, and Bluebirds. I was still a Seagull. I'd watched all the girls but one move over to the Wrens, and then I watched most of them move over to the Bluebirds. The only other girl besides me left in the Seagulls was Lorraine. She was from the village too. But Lorraine was different. At playtime, when the first graders walked up the hill to the big school, and everyone ran from one side of the big gym to the other, playing red rover and dodgeball, Lorraine spun around spun around, full skirt describing a circle, arms held out like Popsicle sticks, black eyes behind thick glasses closed to the gym and to the world. Lorraine didn't play with other kids. She didn't read. That was why she was still a Seagull. But I could read as well as any other girl in the class, even better than some. And I would play if they asked me.

Almost all the other girls were already Bluebirds. Their pink-silk buttoned blouses and woolen winter coats were different from my own unwashed wrinkled cottons. Their scrubbed faces and pigtailed hair made mine feel dirty and drab. Bluebirds moved comfortably and confidently in a world I ventured into timid and alone. At the end of the school day, they were driven back to their picture-book houses for afternoon chocolate chip treats. Like Dick and Jane, they enjoyed snacks of apples and cookies fresh from a clean oven. Fairy-tale spells granted them sugar-coated cookies and homemade cakes decorated with frosting and sprinkles, while I skipped down Village Street hoping for dryfish.

Two girls were still Wrens, but they lived close to the village and sometimes went to school with dirty clothes, as I did almost every day. Like me, they didn't always have money for the *Weekly Reader*. Their moms never baked for the bake sales; my mother was still in the hospital. My grandfather was the only one who baked in our wood-burning stove, and he baked only when he came home from fishing. His flaky biscuits would never suit a bake sale.

We were supposed to advance to the next group when our reading improved, but I suspected that I would also have to dress like Jane and live in a house like hers and have a mom in a white apron rolling cookie dough and decorating cakes for the bake sale and a dad who walked around town holding a dripping umbrella above his head so he wouldn't get wet in the rain.

Everyone stared when I came into class and walked over to the teacher. "I fell down," I whispered.

"Well be careful, now. Try not to drip on the floor. You'd better go up the street to the other school and see the nurse." Mrs. Green shuffled me out the door. "Go on now, dear," she told me. "Go see the nurse. I can't do anything for you with a cut like that."

I walked up the hill holding my eye. The blood now covered my fingers. I could feel it starting to dry. I still hadn't cried. Kaagwaantaan children were strong, my grandmother always admonished. Remember who you are, she told me daily. Kaagwaantaan children don't cry.

At the big school I wandered the empty hall until I saw the nurse's office. I presented myself to the lady in the white dress, the same lady who had poked me and the rest of my classmates with a needle a few weeks before when we lined up for shots. The nurse lifted my hand and frowned. "I can't do anything about this. You're going to need stitches," she said. "Better go to the native hospital, they'll take care of you there. Go along, now."

She guided me out the door. I walked the length of the empty hall still holding my eye. Down the steps and out the building. I could go down the street the way I'd come or I could step down either of the stairways. Or I could walk the long way past the governor's mansion. I walked in the direction of the governor's mansion, looking down on the village with one good eye, down on the dirt street where I'd walked a while ago. If I saw my grandma I would go down the stairs and show her my eye. But Village Street was empty.

Grandma didn't read well, but sometimes she let me read to her about Dick and Jane and their dog, Spot. I showed her the pictures. Grandma was not as intrigued as I by the green lawn in front of the big white house, the red bouncing ball that Spot so happily chased, the sparkling kitchen where Dick and Jane's mom smiled with bright red lips and yellow hair. Sometimes I read from a storybook brought home from school. In it were fairy tales about little girls who had trouble with witches and stepmothers. Alongside the stories were pictures of girls and boys and witches and stepmothers, and pictures of princes. They all looked like they were related to Dick and Jane.

The meaning of the stories was difficult to sort. The most puzzling story was also my favorite, one in which a spoiled, complaining girl, balanced throughout the night atop a pile of mattresses, in the morning was found to be bruised on her fair and delicate skin. Her grumbling brought the recognition that she was after all a princess—she must be, for none but a princess would have had her sleep disturbed by a pea so cleverly placed beneath twenty mattresses. A glistening crown was perched atop her yellow hair, a prince dressed in puffy sleeves and tight pants claimed her hand, and they went to live in a castle with a lawn not unlike Dick and Jane's. It was a mystery how balancing on a pile of mattresses and complaining of a pea would make a princess out of a petulant girl. The answer to this puzzle might cast light on how I could become a Bluebird.

But I didn't learn from those textbook stories the lessons my grandmother already knew. She warned me that no matter what a book or a teacher or anyone else said, I would never be a Bluebird. Nor a Wren. Nor a Seagull. "Never forget," she told me daily, "you are Eagle. Not Raven. Not Seagull. You will always be an Eagle and a Wolf. You will never be a Bluebird."

Past the governor's mansion and down the stairs to Capitol Avenue, through the fenced path across the electric company's property, part of which had once belonged to our family, over a field of wildflowers and bees, into the Native hospital where my mother lived on a forbidden floor in a quarantined ward, I resolutely walked, holding one hand over my eye.

The doctor stitched my eyebrow after the nurse tenderly cleaned it. They told me that my mother knew I was downstairs and was sending me her love right now. They washed my hands and sent me home, where Grandma exclaimed over my stitches. She poked my eyebrow to gauge how much it hurt.

"Did you cry?" she asked.

"No, Grandma," I told her. "I didn't cry."

"Good."

The next morning I found a wrinkled skirt under the wooden cot where I slept, and I tried to smooth it after I put it on. I poured canned milk in a serving-size cardboard box of Rice Krispies my grandfather had given me the last time he came home from fishing. I listened to myself chew. I touched my eyebrow. I wiped my mouth.

On the way to school I saw Paul and showed him my stitches. He gave me a handful of green salmonberries. I took them to be nice. They made my mouth water and my eyes crinkle when I bit them. When Mr. Stevenson saw my bandage, he gave us each a stick of chewing gum. We skipped out the door, bypassing the mean lady and her crabapple trees.

The teacher glanced at me. One of the mothers stood near her, holding her daughter's hand. Nancy, the little girl's name was. We never played together. Nancy tugged away from her mother's hand and ran over to me, her freckled nose wrinkled into a smile. Nancy's eyelashes were red and very pale, like her hair and her skin. She wore a pleated skirt and matching sweater set. Her fingernails were clean, her anklets trimmed with pink scallops on their edges. I was ashamed of my own gray wrinkled socks. I hid my dirty hands.

"Do you want to come to my birthday party?" Nancy asked. "I'm having a party tomorrow and I'm inviting all the girls in the class. Do you want to come?"

"Okay," I said. "I can come."

"Good! Here's where it is." Nancy handed me a drawing of the way to her house. "It's the blue one up the hill from the high school. Number three five one. Tomorrow at three o'clock. Bring me a present!"

All day I worried about the party. Other girls giggled and whispered, but nobody said anything to me. Lorraine wouldn't talk, so there was no one to ask. I wasn't sure what you did at a birthday party. I didn't know what to bring for a present.

The next morning, I sat on the hill behind our old house and picked *yaána.ét*, peeling the strings and biting the green wild celery. I went inside and showed my grandmother the map to Nancy's house. I had decided on my last small box of Rice Krispies as a present.

"I'll walk with you part of the way," Grandma said. We set out up the hill, walking past Evergreen Bowl and through the cemetery. We stopped at the family plot to say hello to my great-grandmother and to my Uncle Benjamin, who had died when he was still a baby. When we walked up the hill and found number three five one, a blue house, Grandma said she didn't like being in the neighborhood and disappeared back down the hill. I sat on the stone wall at the edge of the lawn a distance from the front door and watched a few cars stop. Women and little girls climbed out of the cars holding bright packages with ribbons and bows. I hadn't wrapped my present. Mothers and daughters walked up the pavement and into the house.

I had brushed against one of those mothers at a bake sale. She smelled like an open can of vegetable soup. Her daughter, an unfriendly girl named Barbara, had brought to the bake sale a cake made of magic, frosted with whipped icing and festooned with multicolored sprinkles. When someone said that Barbara had decorated the cake herself, I was as amazed as though I'd been told she could fly. It was one more secret thing that only people who were different from me knew how to do: unknowable, enchanted people who prepared and ate unknowable, enchanted food.

Barbara was the only one who noticed me waiting. She stuck out her tongue and made an ugly face, holding her mother's hand and pulling away. Barbara couldn't read nearly as well as I could, but she was already a Bluebird. She and her mother were among the first to go into the blue house. She carried a bright package, and her mother's shoes clicked on the pavement as they hurried up the walk.

After a while I followed my grandmother's footsteps back down the hill, picking at my bandage as I walked. I thought about the gaily wrapped presents and mothers dressed in angora sweaters and high-heel shoes, long slender fingers with red-painted nails delicately holding their daughters' clean hands. I walked down the hill and back to our old house. The closer I got to the village the happier I felt. Now I could eat my last box of Rice Krispies for tomorrow's breakfast. Before long, I was skipping.

Before giving birth, a Lingít woman sings to her child. She talks to the baby, telling the child the history of her clan and the stories of her people. She describes to the young one in the womb the seasons and the land, the mountains and the rain, the birds, rivers, berries, and the sunsets. The smell of the sky on a blue day. That child is born already loving the land.

When a child is born into this world, the baby is examined for signs that reveal who it truly is. A birth scar might signal that the child is a maternal uncle killed by a deadly blow upon his neck, come back now to rejoin the clan, revealing himself by a dark line upon his collarbone. Or the child might be recognized as her own maternal grandmother, once known for all the piercings on her ears, now seen at this rebirth in the tiny marks on her endearing baby lobes. The signs manifest on its outer side reveal the spirit of the child.

People die. People come, and people go away again. People die. The clan lives on.

Now Raven, once he was born of a woman when the world was still dark. It's told how he changed himself into a pine needle and dropped into the water so an old man's daughter would swallow him. It's told how he changed again inside her belly, and she became pregnant even though she had never known a man. It's told how he was born onto a bed of moss — soft moss dry moss cool moss clean moss forest moss — and how much he was loved by his mother and by his grandfather after he was born.

But it hasn't been told what Raven's mother sang to him when he was in her belly before he was born. What songs did she sing to him, what stories did she tell? With what scars was Raven born?

Of course, this wasn't the first time Raven was born. He was born many times before, and he has been born many times since. Like his own people, he keeps coming back. Like our Lingít Aaní, he keeps coming back. Like the clans, Raven lives on.

Some of those old traditions have now been replaced. Sometimes the singing to the baby in the womb is the crooning of a drunk woman propped up against the side of a building in the cold street, or the loud moan of a country-drunk jukebox in a dim bar. Sometimes the words the unborn innocent hears are the angry shouts of a jealous husband or the raucous laughter of a living room full of thirsty neighbors and two cases of the cheapest beer. Sometimes the lessons the child learns before it is pushed out into an unfriendly world are depression, misery, puke.

These are the scars with which Raven now is born.

Birth. The birth of a child, the birth of Raven. The birth of the new world with the summer's return of the salmon. The young bears come out of their warm hiding places where they listened to their mothers sing to them and tell them the stories of the bear people. Baby birds inside their shells listen to the cries in the air of their fathers and their mothers. They know from the sounds through the shells that the screams of the eagles in the high air, the mimicking of the ravens on the branches, the quiet music of the fearless chickadee, are the stories of their people. They prepare to enter the world. They listen to the songs and the stories so they will be ready. They will be born knowing their own songs and their own stories. They will know their own names.

By the mark, the child's real name is known. By the name, the child is known. Like Raven, the scars we are born with today are not always easily seen.

My mother was born with little piercings on her ears. By this she was known to be her own maternal ancestor; by those marks she was recognized and given her proper name: Kaaxkwéi. I was not born with a recognizable mark. My scars were not on my skin. I was such a hungry baby, my mother said, it was thought that I must be my maternal great-grandmother, who had died the year before I was born and who had not been able to eat at the end of her life. She must have been hungry, it was reasoned. That, my mother told me, was a late indication of who I really was. But by then I had already been given my maternal grandmother's real name, Saankaláxt'. She, too, died before I was born. It was her sister who became my grandmother Saodoo ú. It was Saodoo ú who told me stories; it was she who taught me songs.

Now is the story of Raven.

In the beginning, darkness was upon the world. It was difficult for people to walk around. There was no light. Every time anyone had to go somewhere, they bumped into things. Raven decided to do something about this.

An old man who with his daughter lived apart from all other people was known to own precious bentwood boxes in which were kept all the sources of light. This old man kept those precious boxes to himself and never shared them. Nor did he allow them to be opened. Raven decided to do something about this.

Steambent cedar boxes have many uses. They can be used to store food for the winter: dried herring eggs, dryfish, dried seaweed, berries soaking in seal oil. On long journeys on inside waters, steambent boxes can be used to contain fresh drinking water. Clothing and toys and tools can be stored in plain and marked boxes. Boxes can be sat on. Boxes can be stepped on to make oneself tall enough to pluck from the rafters items that are otherwise out of reach. Fine boxes can be used to contain treasure, such as those boxes that once were used by an old man at the head of the Nass, fine boxes that were used to contain inside them all the light in the world. But when Raven went there to that place on the Nass, he found it impossible to enter the old man's house.

After curious investigation and much thought, Raven transformed himself into a pine needle and dropped himself in that form into water that the old man's daughter was about to drink. She swallowed him, whereupon he transformed himself again, and she became pregnant. After a while a baby was born to the old man's daughter.

It was Raven!

The old man loved his grandchild, as grandparents are known to do. He played with the Raven child and taught him little songs and kept him company. When Raven cried or became upset, the old man did everything he could to quiet him, as grandparents are known to do.

After plenty of time had passed, Raven cried for the precious bentwood boxes. Carved bentwood boxes are painted and decorated with the precise design that fits the particular box. The spirit of the box, and the spirit of what it contains, is manifest on its outer side. It guards the box and its contents. That first box that Raven cried for must have displayed the crest of its contents. The second box must have displayed the crest of its contents. The third box must have displayed the crest of its contents. The spirits must have been strong.

Raven was enchanted by the boxes as well as by their contents. The designs on the boxes were carved and painted according to their contents; the first was of the stars. Black primary outlines fixed the basic form. Red patterns depicted important secondary features. The lines of the designs became wide in places and narrow in places, as they encountered other lines to form shapes that suggested other images. Inside the belly of one crest, the face of an eagle might have kept watch. Inside the belly of another crest, a wolf may have concealed himself. From inside the belly of a third crest, perhaps a raven watched.

When the grandchild Raven cried for the box, the old man at first said no. But Raven kept crying, crying, crying, and the old man finally gave in. That was when Raven opened the first bentwood box, the first box that contained all the stars. Raven played with those stars for a little while. He tossed the stars into the sky. And the world became a little less dark.

Outside, the people must have been startled for a moment. What was that flash? Or perhaps they did not even know a word for flash. Perhaps they had to make up a word for the new thing they had seen, a new word for a thrill they had never before felt.

Raven cried for the next bentwood box. The old man again said no, but

Raven kept crying, crying, crying. The old man finally gave in, and Raven opened the precious box that contained the moon. Raven played with the moon for a little while. Then he tossed the moon into the sky. And the world became a little less dark.

Outside, the people probably hadn't even gotten over their first amazement. They could hardly take another surprise so soon! This time, their stomachs tightened, and a chill shuddered their collarbones. They wanted to run, but where can you run when fear is a blanket? They stood in one place and trembled.

Now the last box was without doubt the finest of all the boxes. Its crest must have been something to see! The spirit that inhabited and protected that box must have been strong and wonderful indeed. But Raven didn't even let that stop him. He cried for the last box. The old man really resisted this time. This was his last box! Would his grandchild never be satisfied? But finally the old man gave in, as grandparents are known always to do, and Raven opened the last precious box. It was this box that contained all the daylight. As light flooded the world, Raven transformed himself into his original form and flew away.

This time, the people were deeply alarmed. This time, even the mountains were frightened.

The cold storage on South Franklin Street was a loud, fishy place where men in bright rubber coveralls stood on large steel tables and slung fish off the boats and into bins, throwing onto the dock the halibut heads that Juneau children harvested for the cheeks. Fried halibut cheeks, boiled salmon heads, and thin soup from an occasional whole fish made up our regular menu. Every few days, my grandmother sent me to a downtown grocery store located where a McDonald's fast food would later squat. Of the three grocery stores within walking distance, this was the only one with a meat counter. I was instructed to ask the butcher for dog scraps. I rushed home with the wrapped meat bone and handed it to my waiting grandmother, who boiled it with onions and potatoes. At dinner I chased the reflection of the kitchen light bulb floating in the greasy soup but never once caught it in my spoon.

When Grandmother made soup, she first set the water to boil in our biggest pot. Only one faucet piped water into the house. In cold weather, the water was kept running. My grandmother wrapped a rag around the faucet to keep it from splashing. She hung a heavy canvas curtain between the kitchen and the front room, and we stayed in the kitchen where the fire in the wood stove and the steam from the pot kept us happy and warm.

After she filled the big pot she put it on the stove, snagging with a metal rod the square-shaped holes, moving aside the smudgy black lids to expose the flame. When she wanted the water to get hot fast she opened a lid and cozied the kettle's bottom inside the stovetop hole, where from my safe perch at the table I could see the flames. Sometimes on that stove she made toast, laying a slice of dry bread on the hot part, turning it over to singe it on both sides. Then she spread butter if we had it and sprinkled the toast with sugar and cinnamon for a special treat that one day I would prepare for my own grandchildren while they sat at my kitchen table watching their grandma at the stove.

We were allowed to hunt deer only in certain places and only in certain seasons when people from an office told us we could. But our need to eat deer meat, and the deer's need to be eaten by us, didn't always follow territorial regulations. So one night late in the fall, my uncles and their friend set me on a folded gunnysack in a red wagon and pulled me over the Douglas Bridge. The night was cold and windy, especially on the bridge. I tried to ask if we were going to visit Aunt Erm and Uncle George and their dog Blackie and if we would pull up chives, the only thing that grew in their garden in the snow, but Uncle Buzz shushed me in a low, threatening whisper and with one word from him I was quiet until we arrived back at our warm, lighted house in the village.

Our house was lighted in the winter, but in summer our electricity ran out and we lived with the daylight. We had no refrigerator, no freezer, no hot water. There was no shower. When I needed a bath, my grandmother heated water in a big pot on the stove and poured it into a tub of cold water until the temperature felt just right to her bared elbow. I climbed or was lifted into the tub, where I sat feeling the newness of looking around the kitchen while sitting naked in warm water. After my bath, my grandmother poured the cooled water into the crank-up washer and tossed in clothes and soap flakes out of a box at the bottom of which we hoped to find a scalloped green plate or teacup and saucer. The big hot-water kettle she used for her chores was the same that she used for soup.

My uncles and their friend pulled me over the bridge and we turned away from Douglas onto the dirt road that went in a direction that was dark and quiet and strange. After a bumpy few minutes we stopped and my Uncle Buzz gently lifted me from the wagon and slid the burlap from under my shivering butt. Skip pulled a gun from the shadows and silently left the road. I stood near the wagon and felt the hairs freezing in my nose and listened to Buzzy and Delphin and the night sounds beside me until I heard the crack of a gunshot. Skip's voice called from the darkness, and at once came the noise of rustling bushes and crunching snow as Buzzy and Delphin rushed in his direction. I stood alone by the wagon until they came back carrying a deer.

Working silently and fast, they folded rich-smelling haunches and clattering ribs and wetly creased skin into the wagon. They covered the deer meat with the now-frozen sack and fit me back on the burlap, where I sat suddenly high like a queen or like one of the princess girls who rode in the cars at the Fourth of July parade, waving from their perches, all sparkles and bubbles and pink. It was from their fathers we were supposed to ask permission when we wanted to hunt for deer meat.

I rocked sideways on my throne, bending to grip the wagon, my boots tucked between the wagon's floor and the warm deer meat that already smelled like tomorrow's soup. Before I knew it we had turned up Capitol Avenue, and I saw our old house up the street across from the million-gallon oil tanks those same office men had put at the side of the village. I jumped off the wagon, uncles and Delphin and deer meat right behind me. Inside the welcoming old house, my grandmother waited in the kitchen with undisguised interest and a sharp knife.

The next day my grandmother fixed soup. After the water was boiling and I'd finished a treat of cinnamon toast, she tossed in the deer meat. She slid the kettle to the back of the stovetop where it was not too hot and let it cook all afternoon. After a while we peeled potatoes.

We didn't buy potatoes at the store. Aunt Erm, my grandfather's sister, grew a good, big garden and didn't mind giving us potatoes now and then. Sometimes carrots and onions. Sometimes turnips and rutabagas that we liked to eat raw. Aunt Erm grew chickens, too, but she never gave us chicken or eggs. They sold the eggs and called them cackleberries. When it was time to kill a chicken, Uncle George held its feet and stepped on its squawking head and chopped its neck with a hatchet, and Aunt Erm cleaned it and cooked it with gravy and noodles and peas. She brought salads and desserts home from the hospital where she worked. She served sauces and gravies I found delicious and new. Her kitchen was a mysterious, industrious place where she did strange things to food besides boil or fry it.

When I was sent to stay with Aunt Erm and Uncle George, I hauled wet seaweed from the beach to feed the garden, weeded the eager potatoes and carrots, fed the cackleberry chickens, and played with Blackie the dog. I looked forward to crunchy fried rabbit, steaming chicken and noodles, fresh vegetables. I loved all the enchanted dishes Aunt Erm served: exotic mashed potatoes; fresh, biting radishes; baked desserts. I associated such foods with the sight of a yellow-haired woman in a frilled apron, like the pictures in magazines and in schoolbooks, and with the unfamiliar smell of hand soap that lingered on Uncle George's fresh-scrubbed hands as we readied ourselves for supper in basins of cold water hauled fresh from the well.

My Aunt Erm was the only one I knew who had a regular job and who lived with a white man who owned a car. She was the only one who always cooked in the manner of white people. The only one whose dinner plates matched. She was part of my family, but she was also part of the other world.

Sometimes I was sent to Aunt Erm's house for a holiday dinner, where things like Easter eggs and fruitcakes were placed on the table as though they were ordinary. In the fashion I had been taught, I made no mention of them and acted as though I didn't notice. When no one was looking, I stared and poked. When it was time to eat, the first nibble of fruitcake or the act of peeling a brightly painted egg allowed me to hope that one day, like the little girl at the bake sale, I would cast sprinkles on enchanted cakes.

But today we had potatoes and we peeled them. After we cut them into bites, my grandmother threw the potatoes into the pot with the deer meat and onions. And carrots. She let it all boil for a little while longer, and then she put in some salt. She carried the pot to the table, where by now Buzzy and Skip and Delphin waited and watched with me. Grandma ladled the soup into our bowls with the big spoon made out of mountain goat horn that was the last thing my grandmother still owned from her own father.

While I waited for the soup to cool in my flat blue Pyrex bowl, I held my face over the steam and inhaled the delicious smell of deer meat stew. The meat scum and grease and gristle floating at the top were going to be good. I blew on the potatoes and judged by the fat and gristle and meat which piece I wanted first. I smiled at my uncles and their friend and listened to their proud stories about hunting for deer meat. I chased the reflection of the kitchen light bulb floating in my greasy soup.

After a while my mother came home from the hospital, and in a few years we left for California. Not long after that, my grandmother died. I wandered in California like a person in a strange dark forest. I saw a woman's grief. I became a stranger. It was a long time before I finally came back home.

Now is the story of Tom's tale.

There'd been a war. They called it a world war. And not the first world war, the teachers said. It was the second world war. World War Two, they named it. Tom heard about it at school, listened to the teachers telling the boys that when they became old enough they would be given guns to fight for their new country, the United States. They heard that Aleut people had been brought to nearby places from their faraway homes in the Aleutian Islands, and the missionary school preacher, Mr. Glasscoe, often talked with his wife about Aleut camps and about the shortage of nylons and chocolate. But none of that meant much to Tom; the changes the war brought to his world were no more surprising than all the other changes placed on him over the years since he was first taken from his family.

As soon as he could hold on to the side of the boat without falling into the water—before he was known as Tom, when he was still called by his Indian name, the name he inherited from his grandfather, Tawnewaysh— his father took him out fishing. No one in the family knew how to swim.

"It's time for you to come with me and fish!" his father had said one glad spring day, pointing in mock surprise at Tawnewaysh. The boy was thrilled when his father aimed his energy at him through one finger, something not to be done in a casual manner. The big man grabbed his five-year-old son under the arms and raised him into the air while the child's mother smiled and held back the laughing baby girls who struggled to join in. "It's time for you to come with your dad and work for the family!"

Tawnewaysh was happy to be fishing alongside his dad during the long summers, steaming into port and selling their fish, making money, returning home to Juneau when summer was over, handing over most of the money to his mom, buying plenty of dry goods at the store, Tang and Spam and pilot bread.

Things were pretty good for him and his two younger sisters, living in the Indian village section of Alaska's capital city. His mom and dad spoke Tlingit around the house and taught him how to catch fish and cut wood and pick seaweed. During winter, a pot of soup warmed them when they came in from hunting deer, sometimes lucky enough to hang one or even two deer in the cold front room curtained off by yellow canvas. After sharing the deer meat with relatives and neighbors, there was often enough to keep for a month or two, frozen in the cache just outside the door. With dried fish and seaweed and deer meat and pilot bread, life was pretty good.

Tawnewaysh looked forward each winter to the coming summer's fishing with his dad, the two of them keeping the engine of the small boat running, finding a spot where they could be sure that the uniformed white men wouldn't find them and give them trouble papers; it had to be a good spot, but not one that was rich enough for white men seiners to take the way they'd taken the land on Douglas Island and out at Auke Bay and up every mountain and down every channel. All Tawnewaysh and his dad needed was a little spot not too far from a town or a cannery. After the girls got a little older, the whole family came along, and then it was even more fun, fishing and berrypicking all summer, pulling the boat onto the shores and smoking or drying fish for themselves, fishing some more and taking the haul to a cannery now and then for cash.

At the end of one summer, when he was ten years old by white man's counting, a white lady dressed in a shiny gray skirt and an unfriendly jacket climbed out of a car in front of the house and knocked on the door. Tawnewaysh was taken away to a missionary boarding school in another town. The missionary's wife took away his clothes and made him dress in a buttoned shirt and stiff pants. The missionary and his wife took away his old name and gave him a new one. Tom. Now he was called Tom.

Haines House wasn't too bad. As soon as he remembered not to speak Tlingit but only English, and learned to keep his uncomfortable clothes buttoned up to his neck even though it choked him, and as soon as he remembered to pray at least five times every day, kneeling by the wooden chair, elbows on the seat, head bent, eyes squinted shut, face crumpled into the earnest frown that he knew the white men's god liked best, listening as the white man preacher went on and on and on until the boy was dizzy and sweaty and hungry enough to eat even the thin, unhappy vegetables grown in the outside gardens, boiled and stewed and mushed into a dish for lunch and dinner, as soon as he got used to being called Tom instead of Tawnewaysh, it wasn't too bad at Haines House.

He missed his dad and mom and his sisters for a long time. They came to see him at first, but the white man preacher wouldn't let them visit. When he saw his family through the window, he tried to run outside and hug his mom, but the white lady teacher stopped him. When he fought, she called for help, and the preacher came with his tall grown son and they carried Tom to the back of the hall into the preacher's office, where the preacher made Tom bend down and pray, and at the end of the long amen they sent him to bed without any supper and without a hug or a visit from his mom, congratulating themselves at the next Sunday's pulpit that they were right not to let Native children see their families for at least a year while they busied themselves working hard to take the Indian out of the child.

For the first few months, Tawnewaysh consoled himself to sleep with the image of his mother standing at the gate on the fenced lawn, a dark blanket wrapped around her shoulders, breeze and light rain moving her long hair, his sisters at her side, his father standing behind her, holding her bent elbows in his hands, his chin on her shoulder, all of them gazing toward the window where he stood poised on the brink of their lives, ready to run. Only one year after he was sent to Haines House, Tom learned that his sisters had started going to school right there in Juneau, and were learning to speak English, dressing in hand-me-down clothes from charitable white churches. By then Tom didn't care enough to wonder why they didn't let him go back home. By then he'd made some friends, and he'd learned how to lie and how to laugh at the preacher's prissy, clean hands and how to take a whipping and pray for an hour when he was being punished. By then he'd become Tom, and Haines House wasn't so bad.

When he was fifteen years old by white men's ways, which were now his ways as well—at least the counting and language and money and church-going parts of being white, and the lying and the sneaking and believing the constant lessons that the white man and all his ways were infinitely better than any Native way—Tom was sent to Sheldon Jackson School in Sitka. At Haines House, his main jobs had been working in the vegetable garden, sweeping, mopping, and waxing floors in the public rooms, and cranking the washing machines every day. He worked most of the day on his chores, and two or three hours each day on his lessons. Some of his friends worked in the kitchen or as personal assistants to the preacher or his wife. Everyone took turns washing dishes, and everyone took turns serving. But at Sheldon Jackson School, all the boys and girls were expected to learn a craft that would allow them to make a living, such as sewing or cooking. All the jobs they were offered had to do with being a servant. Tom was assigned the chore of learning to be a carpenter.

Of course he'd rather fish. Although his old name and his old language and his old food and his old way of dressing had been slapped and lectured out of him, he remembered the feel of a boat on the water, crisp air, killer whales and jumping fish and cold ocean spray. He remembered those days with his dad, and the whole family stopping to smoke fish and pick berries and take pleasure in living the life they were meant to live, the life it was best for them to live, the life they needed to live in order to be fully themselves. Tom remembered everything about those young days, and learning to nail boards and fasten hinges and fix windows for the white lady teacher so she could catch a breeze through her lacy curtains while she pincurled her hennaed hair was an unsatisfactory substitute for taking his place in a long, long line of men who were meant to fish.

At the edge of an upwelling spring, a bear waits. She dips her curious nose into the stream, hoping to catch the underwater promise of salmon coming closer coming closer coming close. The sun tells her the time is near. The grasses tell her the time is near. Other bears, who take their places up and down and alongside and in and on every stream every river every waterfall, tell her the time is near.

It is almost time for the salmon to return.

Inside their fat bellies, the salmon carry eggs. The bear smells them. She hopes for a fat salmon, its belly full of eggs and its fat brains and delicious fat skin wriggling its way into her hungry waiting mouth. On lucky days, the salmon jump into her hungry waiting mouth.

Standing at the fall, she snaps her jaw shut over a fish that has jumped into her mouth. She drools in anticipation of the delicious taste of the fat and skin and eggs of the fish struggling between her teeth. She concentrates so she won't drop it. She centers her attention on the fighting fish. It fights for its life. She holds it tightly. She clamps down.

She scrambles uphill over the slippery rocks at the shore. She drops the fish into a pool of dirt and holds it with one paw. She looks around her. She sees no threat. She bites the head of the fish. She tastes its skin and its brain. She tastes its fat. She drools.

Her two cubs run up and grab parts of the still-flopping fish with their sharp little young bear teeth. She peels the skin in strips from the salmon while her babies watch. She chews on the skin. She drools. She continues this until most of the skin is gone, the excited cubs smelling her mouth and the fish and the shining strips of skin that hang from her jaw. She looks around her for any threat. Other bears are trying their luck in the stream, and so far she is still safe. She bites the belly of the fish.

The bright orange eggs pop in her mouth. She smiles.

When my mother came home from the hospital, she found me happy and limping. "It's just growing pains," my grandmother told her. "Just wait. She'll grow out of it."

But my mother, whose faith in hospitals hadn't diminished even though working in a tuberculosis ward had resulted in the loss of half a lung and a long recuperation away from her family, took me back to that same green-trimmed, square white building where she had begun her tubercular journey, and listened to the white doctor explain rheumatic fever.

I was taken out of school and set on the couch in the front room, now kept constantly warm for my comfort and pleasure. My mother found work cleaning offices. The doctor instructed her not to allow me any strenuous activity. I abandoned girlish cartwheels and backbends and enjoyed my life on the couch. When Valentine's Day came — the day I had once dreaded for its uncertainty, knowing my own poor heart-shaped offerings would never measure up to the elaborate white-lace constructions of my classmates, knowing the few cards that bore my scribbled name would never compete with the dozens inscribed to the popular Bluebird girls, knowing above all that if I sent a card to someone who did not return the gesture I would be the subject of laughter, something my grandmother had taught me I must never allow — my mother came home with a bag full of valentines from everyone in third grade.

Every valentine card whispered that I was special, now that I had been weakened by this condition of the heart; when I unfolded a handmade card from my teacher, a white lady I'd thought had never liked me, I found a Hershey's bar taped to bright-pink paper with the words "You are as sweet as" penned with apparent affection above the candy. It convinced me that being trapped on the couch in the front room of our old house was a small, small price for the popularity I had thought would never be mine.

Later that spring, my tonsils were removed at Saint Ann's Hospital. It was special treatment for a Native child to be seen at that hospital, but the doctors made an exception because of the fever in my heart. White-capped nurses strapped me to a gurney and covered my face with the mask my mother had told me to expect. I breathed in the gassy poison and counted backward from one hundred almost to ninety. My red ether dreams featured a Ferris wheel staircase up which the white-jacketed doctor and I slowly climbed, holding hands and making no progress, while he spoke to me in loud, simple words, explaining things we both knew only he could understand.

The following year, my mother and I moved to Tacoma for a BIA-sponsored year-long clerical course. We lived with her brother and his wife. Uncle Eugene and Aunt Melba were blind. Melba had a seeing eye dog named Gypsy; Eugene used only a white cane. Uncle Eugene was over six feet tall and had been a star of track and field at Sitka's Sheldon Jackson School before he was blinded by disease. Aunt Melba, a Bristol Bay woman from a group termed *Eskimo* in those days, was less than five feet tall and had been blind since birth. Together they presented an oddity that the neighbors were willing quietly to tolerate.

When my mother and I moved into their spare bedroom it disrupted not only Melba's and Eugene's reserved lives but also the community dynamics. My attendance at the elementary school uphill from Uncle Eugene and Aunt Melba's house became fourth-grade torture; when the well-meaning teacher pointed me out on the first day as the new little Native girl from the territory of Alaska, I fidgeted and blushed under the silent stares of my light-skinned classmates. On the playground, boys teased and chased me while the girls ignored or shoved me. Before long, I routinely made myself sick with worry and begged my mother every morning to excuse me from school.

My stomach ached daily. The mornings that my mother walked with me to consult the teacher were worst of all. Alone, the only Native student in the whole school, friendless, living down the street with a scowling mother, a blind uncle and an aunt who walked with a seeing eye dog, I could only submit to my fate as I had once submitted to a red dream of poisonous ether.

At the end of the year, my mother completed her secretarial course at the business school and we hightailed it back to Juneau, where she began working in an office. We stayed at the old house in the village for only a few months. My grandmother and grandfather by now were drinking more than ever, my uncles were older but still living at home, my Aunt Ida had already moved out. My grandmother had abandoned cooking, cleaning, raising children. My mother and I moved to a small apartment, where we lived by ourselves, visiting my grandmother frequently and Aunt Erm every few days.

For my mother, cooking was mostly a matter of boiling or frying. She fried salmon or halibut or halibut cheeks. Rice was the staple; fried potatoes cut up with wiener nickels offered an interesting change when she felt like taking the time. Canned corned beef either stirred into a frying pan and mixed with hot sticky rice or boiled with potatoes into a canned tomato stew, canned Spam with canned sweet potatoes, fried cabbage with bacon, and hamburger served with dark brown canned gravy poured over rice rounded out her repertoire. Canned cream corn was our favorite vegetable. Once in a while we enjoyed fried liver covered with fried bacon and fried onions. Now and then for a special treat she served up a fried beefsteak. Thrown into a hot frying pan with smoking bacon grease, the round steak sizzled while she prepared a salad. She cut lettuce, a fresh delicacy, into bites, sliced tomatoes into wedges, and mixed the whole thing with mayonnaise. With a busy frown, she turned the steaks in the smoking pan, checked the rice, and occasionally scrambled eggs for a special side dish. She roasted and garnished only on Thanksgiving day in a marathon session that included turkey and bread stuffing, Cheez Whiz spread into sliced fresh celery, and mashed mustard-flavored egg yolk piled into hardboiled whites. Pickles and black olives finished the festive meal; our dessert was store-bought pumpkin pie squirted with whipped cream.

Once in a while somebody gave us Native food; now and then we stayed for dinner at Aunt Erm's house across the channel. But mostly we ate my mother's version of American cooking while we tried out our first tentative steps, readying ourselves to take our place in the white man's world now that she had learned how to type.

The year after he started at Sheldon Jackson, Tom and a friend went back to Juneau for a visit. His friend, who'd been given the name Sam, was related to the family who lived two houses down from Tom in the Indian village around which the town of Juneau had grown. Tom was sixteen. His dress-up white man trousers hung to his ankles, showing clean white socks and polished brown shoes aching his feet below the let-out creased hem of his pants. Susie, Sam's cousin, was four years older than Tom and already worked at a cannery during the summer and at a local café during the winter, a café that allowed Native men and women to work as staff and even welcomed Natives and Filipino people as customers.

Susie was a handsome girl and had no time for Tom. He learned that she'd been a waitress at the local café for a couple of years and had been friendly with Coast Guard and other military men stationed in town. Now that the war was over, her sphere of friends was more limited, but she still seemed busy and popular to Tom's admiring eyes. Tom and Sam stayed in Juneau for less than a week, dizzy and dazzled at the fast pace and bright lights. Tom's visit with his folks was strained and uncomfortable, the house crowded and the food meager. On the night before he was to leave, his mother sat with him at the wooden table after a thin supper of fish soup. She held a cup of steaming Hudson Bay tea, smoothing the tip of her finger against the chipped ceramic edge with each sigh and each word.

"You've grown so much, Tawnewaysh."

"I'm Tom now. It's the modern way."

"I know. I'm sorry, I think of you as the boy you were when they took you. I wish you hadn't gone." Her voice trailed off. She picked at a hangnail on her finger, biting and drawing blood. "We tried to stop them. We tried to get you back, but they wouldn't even let us talk to you."

"It's all right. I eat good, they're teaching me to make things from wood.

Why isn't Dad still fishing?" Tom had wondered about the boat, had seen that it seemed in ill repair.

"His back bothers him, and he needs more help than he can get. He's thinking about taking us down to Tacoma so he can go to school and learn a trade there. He thinks I can learn to type. We could get better jobs and live easy."

"That would be good. You could take better care of yourself, buy more food, get the girls new clothes."

"I don't want to leave until you finish with the school. That way, maybe you could come with us." She touched Tom's hand with the tip of a bitten finger, tracing the line of his workingman's hand. "You're almost a man now."

"When I finish school the preacher says I should join the army. He says I'll be better off, and I'll have a chance to see the world."

"I wish you would never leave, I wish none of us would ever leave. If we could just keep living and fishing it would be good." She looked up as Tom's dad came into the room. He sat at the table with a sigh and a thump, frowning. "Are you all right?" she asked.

"My back. It's the same." He sat straight like an upright pole.

"Tom says they want him to join the army when he finishes with school. If he does that, he won't be able to go with us if we move to Tacoma."

"Whatever they think he should do, that's probably what he should do." He looked at Tom. "What do you want to do, son?"

Tom agreed with his mother. He wished no one had to go anywhere. He wished he'd never been taken away to boarding school. He wished he could still fish with his dad on the family boat, save him from hard work and heavy lifting, show him that he was becoming a strong, good man. He wished everything could be different.

"I don't know," he told his father. "I guess I should sign up for the army before they come and get me, like the preacher says."

His father grunted. "I suppose you should do what they tell you," he said. "Fishing will be all gone soon enough, anyway. So will the hunting. They already tell us where we can fish and what we can hunt, while they give away land that should have been our home forever." His voice lowered, and Tom strained to hear and understand his father's words. "They won't stop until they do the same things to us that they did to their own Jesus. They beat us and break the land and then they crucify us. After that they worship it all." He pointed a bent finger at his disconcerted son. "Listen to me, Tawnewaysh. These white people kill something, and then they love it. They run us over, and they run the land over, and they take what they want, and when they got us beat they plant a fence around everything and say that it's all theirs." He covered his face with cheerless hands. His words choked through ragged fingers. "Our land," he moaned. "Our forest. Our fish. Our stories." With one more ragged sigh he dropped his hands. "Remember, boy," he said. "Whatever they do to the land they'll do to us."

It was already after the day that Raven dropped the land from his mouth; that was long before. It was also after the day that Raven spit out the rivers and streams onto the land—that too was long before. And it was well after the day that Raven brought daylight into the world. It was the midnight of the long-ago day when the glaciers began to retreat.

It takes a measured while to do such a thing. The glaciers' retreat this time was not as rapid as had been their advance. When the glaciers decided to advance, they did so in a rush. Often they ran, chasing things. But when the time was full, when after how long how long they had pushed so close so close to the sea, but didn't make it all the way—they'd pushed so close but always there had been that edge of land, some plants, some trees, a few caves, always a stretch of beach—they couldn't quite cover it all. After pushing as hard as they could for as long as they could, finally they gave up. They stopped pushing. They rested—just a short while for a glacier, only a little while in Raven time—and began to back up. Slowly in most cases. Bit by bit.

At that midnight, when the night turned over in its sleep, the edge of never-covered land was almost bare. Parts of the land sticking out from under the lips of glaciers here and there were crusted black with cold. Only tufts of moss grew on alpinelike land near the lengths of unruly beaches. But not far from those long beaches, the intertidal community was rich.

Farther out, the deep ocean made an abundant home for the rich plankton that bloomed each annual cycle in a swimming curtain thick enough to call herring and crab and whales from their farthest winter homes. The low sea level made of the beaches long dank expanses of living and dying and dead muck and slime and drifted wood and seeds from warmer shores.

The glaciers waited, planning capitulation.

Cold water from the glaciers pushed the warmer surface water toward the deeper ocean. Warm water hiding below rose to replace its colder other self. Silt and dirt and seeds and wood and rocks and stones scraped loose by the advancing ice and carried to the rocks near the shore fell into the water with loud thundering splashes, exciting nearby birds, who watched for just such a thing to disturb the underside of the water and urge plants and plankton and shellfish buried in sands below the waterline to rise and feed the waiting birds.

Shorebirds, bellies filled, flew heavily to the beach, where their digestion dropped onto the newly exposed ground the seeds and nutrition from past and recent feasts. At the right time, the birds built rough nests on the rocks and on the beach, and the females squatted to deposit their eggs onto the hard ground and warmed them with soft bellies.

The birds didn't use their nests for long. They stayed on those eggs for little more than a cycle of the moon. But that was long enough to notice that the ice was already farther away than when they'd first come to this place. By the time the eggs began to make croaking noises from inside, and then pecking noises, and then to display little cracks and then bigger cracks and then a whole baby bird's beak and eyes and head, and finally a wet scrawny birdchild, the ice was even farther away.

By the end of the first summer season after that long-ago day when the glaciers decided to retreat, the edge of the ice had almost reached the island's inside coast. For the space of one winter and then into spring and then to summer, that ice rested in a cold, wet land, and against its own will it advanced a little space, and with the next warming season continued its retreat. The uncovered land appeared meager, but held within it all the life, all the promise, all the seeds of our own future yet unborn.

A child waited in her mother's womb, listening to the stories and the songs of her clan and to the music of the land. Already she held within her all the life, all the promise, all the seeds of the clan. Already her mother taught her, transferring to her the future. Already she was protected.

Her mother held her. Her mother was careful not to take fright, nor to look at anything strange, nor to eat food fresh from the beach. Only dryfish. Only seaweed. Only berries.

The child was not yet a full person. It was not yet revealed who she was. Within her was all the future, but as yet there was no present. This is the way it was with the land when the glacier began again to retreat in the next warming season. This was how it was when the newly uncovered land sent out its invitation: Come now! Come sing, come dance, come eat! Come now!

There were times when the glaciers backed away more quickly from the edge of the long tideland beach. As richly as the seawater bloomed with plankton resting in the comfort of the cold water, as richly as the baby girl bloomed with ears to hear songs and eyes to see loved places and fingers with which to delicately pick one small berry and crush it into her waiting open mouth, so did the land bloom with the seeds inside and just under its skin. Beach grass and mosses and lichen and shrubs. Seeds unburied, seeds spread by shorebirds, seeds carried by the melting ice. Sprouting, growing, blooming. Like the plankton. Like the girl. Like the land.

The ice retreated fast at times. Its melting water rushed to the ocean, where warm water rose to displace the ice water and to push it out to sea. With it the deep water carried life from below. That life bloomed and lived near the shore and was carried farther with the streaming ice water. This life bloomed. This life fed the larger shellfish driven up from the bottom. This life called from far distances fish and seals and whales. It wasn't long in Raven time before the rhythm of the world had changed, before the song of this part of the earth, the song of this land, had risen once again to the loud chorus of praise and richness in which increasing numbers of people and their relatives would one day again rejoice.

Soon growing things covered the land, growing from once-covered seeds and nourished by increasing rains. Before long, a salt marsh covered the land near the shore. Farther back, a beach meadow bloomed, covered at first with grasses and moss and ferns and shrubs. Birds made use of grasses for their nests. More shrubs began to grow. Willow and alder trees here and there caught hold in the scraped and wakening dirt. After the willows and alder became a little taller, they made shade. In the shade, the ground stayed moist. The roots of the shrubs and trees loosened the earth. It felt good for the tightly packed earth to be loosened, now that the weight of the ice no longer pressed it down. Devil's club took root. Skunk cabbage woke. Fireweed sprang up everywhere.

In another season, all the children of the fireweed covered the whole length of the shore and inward, dancing with lupine and thistle and here and there a happy buttercup. Each summer, the island was abloom with the children and the grandchildren of all the fireweed.

In not many more seasons, berries choked out as much as they could. Blushing strawberries in the salt marsh near the shore. Quick-witted Jacob berries in the shade of the bushes in the beach meadow. Blueberries and salmonberries and thimbleberries. Soapberries and raspberries. Huckle-berries. All this from the droppings of happy birds. The ice had completely withdrawn from this part of the land. The birds made their homes here. The few creatures who had been here when the ice came almost to the shore were also content. Finally! Abundance! Berries, greens, birds in great numbers! But the berries and grasses attracted more than the birds. Already-curious and always-hungry animals came from farther shores. Strong swimmers. Young. Ready to hunt and to eat.

With the spring came young, green plants, beach grass, the tender buds and shoots that coaxed awake the digestion of any hungry bear only recently stirred by the calls of vigorous birds and the smell of warm spring breezes. Out from her den came the brown bear. Out from slumber came her dreams. Were those pictures in her mind only the stuff of sleep, or were they her memories? Memories of a future time, a time when she was human. Memories of a distant place, a woman's brothers, a song. Memories of what might never be. But for now, her hunger drove her to the sedge, to a taste of green that rumbled in her belly and forced her to the beach, where she busied herself digging for clams and rooting for barnacles, and gazed toward the endless ocean while she thoughtfully chewed.

She noticed birds soaring in the blue air. She heard their calls. She inhaled the smell of a distant sea lion. She felt the wind on her still-sleepy face. She smelled the fragrance of faraway fish. She waited.

It is midnight. The female salmon noses the river bottom, testing the gravel for a place she likes. She hesitates at a spot in the fresh current and finds a place to make a nest. She shivers her tail in the understream gravel, and as the cool water washes her reddening face she indents an impression. She situates herself over the dimple. She turns on her side and slaps the gravel with her tail. She pushes. She pushes thousands of eggs into the nest she has made. She has captured the attention of the battling males. She pushes.

A victorious red male, ferocious and irresistible, joins her. Together they quiver and gape. He fertilizes her eggs, not waiting for her to finish. Their bodies tremble as the last of her orange, clustered eggs and the last of his white, milky sperm join in a spasm. Finished, he swims away to die. Finished, she covers her eggs with the last of her strength, and she swims away to die. With good luck the male and female will die in this stream where they, too, once were buried as eggs under the gravel, where the bodies of their own ancestors once nourished their own early growth. With good luck they will die here in this deep, moving water. With good luck their bodies will nourish the eggs that now contain all their hopes for the future.

The year begins with the salmon's summer return. The salmon return to spawn and to die. The year begins with the death of the salmon. But first, before they die, the salmon put the next generation in place. And then they die. And the year begins. It is finally the moon of the salmon's return, and now the year begins.

It is said that long ago the salmon-people held a race to see who would get the best streams. They came as fast as they could in their canoes. The chinook was the winner of the race. So the chinook salmon-people got the best rivers, the biggest rivers. Next came the sockeye. The sockeye picked lakes and good streams. Then came the pink salmon, they picked good rivers and streams where they can go to lay their eggs. After that came the coho, they claimed waters close to the coast and tributaries. Last of all, because they kept going back, came the dog-salmon people. But instead of winning the least prize, there was no particular stream left for them at all. Thus they lay their eggs anywhere they can. They use every kind of stream for a place to deposit their eggs, even the tidewater. The results of this race can still be seen in the pattern of their return each year.

Salmon gather at the mouth of the stream. Each stream, each river, is claimed by a particular clan. The first salmon to appear is often the chum, the one that lost the race. They go everywhere, and for the longest time. Theirs is the best meat to eat fresh.

When the first salmon returns, the clans don't forget to thank the salmon-people for coming back again. The first salmon is greeted, welcomed, treated like a guest. The first salmon is put back in the water so he will go tell the rest of his people that he was treated well, and there is no reason for them not to return.

Then the catching begins. Many, many salmon are caught, using dip nets and weirs. At first, their flesh is eaten fresh, because it has been such a long time since the people had a taste of fresh salmon. Roasted. Boiled. Steamed. Their eggs (they are full of eggs, small, pink, meaty, tasty handfuls of eggs in the bellies of the best ones) are mixed with cooked seaweed and eaten along with the meat of the fish. Salmon heads are boiled; the gristly nose goes to a lucky child. And to the oldest person goes the mushy cheek, so soft that teeth aren't needed to gain well-being from its flavor. The oldest person presses the morsel with her tongue, reliving salmon days of long ago. With her wrinkled finger, she saves a tiny piece of the softest part and places it gently into the rosebud mouth of a waiting baby, who grimaces in pleasure at this, the first delicious taste of the substance of her people.

With the return of the salmon, the year begins anew. Homesick salmon gather at the mouths of the streams and rivers that poured them into the world. They ready themselves for a last mighty effort. Inside the females, eggs make their bellies fat. Males take on the fierce faces and nature that will give them the best chance to endure. Fish tails waving, they wait for the mysterious signal that tells them, Now! and they swim into the stream, fighting the current, fighting the waiting, grateful people, fighting the hungry bears, fighting one another, fighting death.

The Emerging Forest

When the sun is about to set and you find yourself still in the forest, take care. Stop walking. Stand still. Look around you.

You will see that the shadows are becoming long. This is the time that trees think about telling you things you don't know. While they are considering how much to tell you, there is still time for you to consider your path. Look around. Take care. While you study your surroundings for a likely retreat, keep a watchful eye for other signs. Other marks. Other declarations. In the opposite direction from the way you should go, you might see some chips of wood at the foot of a tree. Especially if it is cedar. Especially if it is yellow cedar. Especially if the sun is about to set.

If you are a fool or if you are bold, you might not be able to resist walking toward those scraps of wood that seem to shimmer in the faded shadowing light. If you are lucky, you might grab a handful. At once their taste will fill your mouth. At once your hands will itch, and you will squeeze that handful tightly. You will stand suddenly and run in the opposite direction. Or at least we can hope it will be in the opposite direction.

You might run all the way back to where you live. You might grip that handful of wood chips so hard that your grandmother will have to pry your fingers open while your uncles hold you down. Suddenly you will let go. You can't fight your own grandmother. They will step back in wonder when they see what you hold. From that day forward, you will always be rich.

In my mother's later years, when I knocked on her apartment door, I often wished for a pot of boiled canned corned beef, quickly poured tomato sauce to spice it, sliced onions and potatoes simmering an invitation. My own attempts at motherhood had included home-cooked meals; my kitchen often filled itself with the crackle and aroma of pot roasts and dumplings, cream sauces and breads. Decorated cookies baked with ginger and festooned with chocolate-chip buttons danced along the cooling rack, homemade granola rich with wheat germ and rolled oats filled the jars, to be served topped with natural honey I all but collected from the bees.

A well-kept house with clean floors was another maternal ideal absorbed from magazines and my imagination. Washing supper dishes and wiping the counter had been the extent of my own mother's housekeeping. When I was young she now and then swept the floor, and in later years might occasionally defrost the refrigerator. Fine points such as waxing or polishing were not in our world. Hanging paintings to enliven the walls or tying ruffled curtains on sparkling windows was completely outside any frame in our reference.

My own attempts to polish and conscientiously clean, like my cooking, fizzled as soon as I no longer had to provide a home for my children. It turned out to have been something foreign carried out in feeble imitation of the pictures in my mind: a lipsticked woman in a sparkling, well-kept kitchen humming while she removed cookies from the oven, a starchy, fresh white apron tied in a big bow, one ear cocked for the glad sounds of clean and happy children skipping home from a popular day at school, ready for a glass of milk with which to make a funny moustache.

I hear in others' voices a smug regard as they lightly complain about such things as shopping with Mom or tolerating a motherly tidying of their rebel-messy apartments. Advice was a commodity never traded in our world, the world only we two inhabited. No brothers, no sisters. No husband, no father. Cousins long gone, aunts and uncles removed. Fled to a foreign California, there to be abandoned to my own life, cast upon the waters with no more anchor than I had ever felt, she finally able to respond to the calls of other places without concern, to leave me to my life, while at last she searched for her own.

Tom made it back to Juneau in 1949, bedraggled, sore, and broke. He was still strong, though. Still able to put in a good day's work on a boat. He still knew how to repair a boat and string a line. He remembered all those lessons from boyhood, although sometimes he felt like he'd forgotten something important.

When he walked up the flat dirt street to the family house in the village and tried the door, he was surprised to find it blocked. The house looked empty. Walking around the sides of the house, he saw that one window was broken, another left open. He circled the house, calling, until a face appeared in a window two doors down the street and out the door came Susie, holding a hammer.

She looked even more handsome than she had those years before. Her thick black hair was curled in the style of the day, rolled into a frame for her cheekboned face, full lips still smeared with the morning's lipstick. Tom waited until she walked up to him, until she had made clear by her actions that she'd come out not to assault him but to talk. She drew close with a frown on top of a worried smile.

"Your folks are gone," she told him. "They left town almost two years ago, right after they heard you joined the army." She gestured with her arms, as if to indicate emptiness. "They're gone," she repeated, and waited for him to understand.

"Gone?" he could only say. "Where did they go?" He looked around in the direction she gestured, confirming for himself her cold, vacant words. "Who lives here now?"

"Nobody. They boarded it up last year after people kept going inside and drinking and starting fires. You can use this if you want to get in." Susie handed him the hammer and sat on the front steps, brushing off a spot next to her to pat an invitation. "Your family went stateside. Your dad's back got so bad they thought they could go around Tacoma so your mom could go to school. They said they'd be back in a year, but they've been gone for two years now, and they didn't come back yet."

Tom was confounded at this unexpected circumstance, but he was quick to recognize a chance to sit next to a healthy young woman. He made himself comfortable where she'd swept a spot for him, widening his legs just a little bit to nudge her incautious knee. "Well," he began. The bone of her kneecap rubbed through the fabrics of his chinos and her blue jeans. A shiver ran up his thigh.

He'd been with only two women. Both had been prostitutes in San Francisco where he'd been sent when he enlisted in the army almost three years ago. The first had been a tired old painted-up white woman he'd given ten dollars when he went out on a bender the first time he got leave. She'd made quick work of him and his ten dollars, and then she had tried to hang on to him and the rest of his money. Dissatisfied and disappointed, he ditched her pretty fast but then had kept drinking. He hardly remembered one whole hour of the next three weeks.

The second woman was a few months later, after he'd been dishonorably discharged for being AWOL. Altogether his whole military experience had taken about a year and a half—not counting the twenty minutes with the second woman, who was also a tired old white woman. He'd never been with a Native woman.

"So what are you doing these days?" he asked Susie. He leaned against the step, trying to look casual and untroubled.

"I'm working," she said. "I work at the hospital now, in the TB ward." She looked in the direction of the hospital, across the field, over the creek. "I'm off today."

"I need to get a job, too," Tom told her, "but I'll probably try to fish. Do you know what happened to our boat?"

"I think it got sold so your folks could pay their way to Seattle."

Tom was disappointed. "Well, that's okay, I guess," he said. "I can sign on with somebody else. Or maybe get work in the cold storage." He turned to look directly into her eyes, a trick he'd learned from listening to the guys in the army. He smiled. "What are you doing later?"

She smiled back and patted his eager knee. He didn't like the older-sister way she touched him. "I'm washing clothes and getting ready for work. Today was my day off. I go back to work tomorrow." She stood and tapped his shoulder. "If you need anything, let me know. I'll help you, okay?" She walked back to her house.

"Thanks!" Tom called. "I'll let you know!" He picked up the hammer and knocked open the door with a couple of two-fisted blows, hoping she noticed and was impressed by his force.

Inside, the bare wood smelled like piss and old liquor. The windows had all been boarded up, the few pieces of furniture tipped over—a broken chair, a bent table, a bed. Rags and broken bottles lay near the stove. The toilet in the small stall was filled with shit and wouldn't flush. The dry faucet at the sink in the kitchen didn't even shudder when he tried the handle.

Tom needed work so he could fix up the house. He needed food, water piped in. He needed a blanket, firewood, pilot bread, Tang. He needed a woman.

He spent a little of the money he had left at Stevenson's Market, up the street from the village. He said hello to Mr. Stevenson, who was still the friendly old man Tom remembered from early boyhood. Tom and his dad would sometimes stop in at the market on their way home from a fishing trip and buy a melon or a pastry as a surprise for the family. Even though he was a white man, Mr. Stevenson always gave them respect, letting them take their time deciding and not following them around while they lingered over their many choices. Except for a few more lines on his face and a more crooked stoop to his shoulders, Mr. Stevenson was the same nice old guy. He recognized Tom right away.

"Well, Tawnewaysh! Or should I say Tom! How are you, boy?" Mr. Stevenson clapped the counter in a noisy greeting. "Are your folks back with you?"

"No, I'm alone, Mr. Stevenson. I caught a fishing boat out of Seattle and got into town this morning. I didn't even know they were gone."

"Well, that's too bad, son. Are you staying in town, moving back to your old place?"

"That's what I'm hoping to do."

"Well, you let me know if you need some credit while you get on your feet. That goes for your folks, too, if they show up. They were always good people, far as I'm concerned." He picked a Baby Ruth bar from under the counter, pushing it toward Tom. "Fishing's been pretty good," he went on. "Unless you're planning to do something different, put some of that learning of yours to work?"

Tom took the candy and nodded in thanks. In the old days, Mr. Stevenson could always be expected to offer a free treat to a wide-eyed boy. "No, nothing's better than fishing, Mr. Stevenson." Tom tucked the Baby Ruth in an inside pocket, patted it for good measure. "I'll be getting on the first boat that'll have me."

"You won't have any trouble, boy. You let me know if I can help."

Tom picked out a few things, paid cash and carried them back to the house. He stopped at the Salvation Army church along the way for cleaning rags and blankets. They gave him what he needed and invited him back for a meal after service on Sunday. Tom took his load of supplies up the street to the house and cleaned the floors and unboarded the windows. He collected some wood and started a little fire in the kitchen stove. He took the Baby Ruth sweet bar from his jacket pocket and, watching the fire, slowly peeled off the colorful wrapper. Its candy-coated smell woke up the hairs in his nose. Its slippery brown bumpiness softened his fingers. He licked the taste off his thumb and bit a piece of the chocolate sweet. Its sharp taste flooded his unsuspecting mouth with eager saliva. He chewed the chocolate nut caramel and warmed himself near the fire. In the gradual dark he made his hopeful plans.

My mother's unwatchful style of raising me had stood us in adequate stead while I skipped through childhood. But when I turned thirteen, a precocious half-breed girl in a territory full of men, the absence of motherly advice combined with other factors to make quick work of my innocence. When a boy from the white neighborhood stole a bottle of something he called burgundy from his parents' supply and invited my best friend

Willa and me underneath the bleachers for a taste of the sick-sweet liquor, I began a headlong walk down the long, long path that virtually every Native person I knew had also walked.

Both the boy and my friend Willa were older than I, but neither of them was Native. The boy was given a slap on the hand and told never to speak to me again. Willa was put on a year's probation and invited to live in the probation officer's home. It might have seemed a favorable placement; Willa was a white girl but she lived near the village in a ramshackle apartment building with her fat ill-bred mother, her vague and insubstantial father, and a raft of rowdy brothers and sisters. An obscene roll of thick, uncut bologna predictably cluttered the unwiped counter of their dirty kitchen; a bottle of ketchup ordinarily lay on its side next to the bologna, waiting to be slapped on a slice of white bread and eaten in the bathroom while Willa checked on the captured frogs she kept in the tub. On the front porch, we walked through dried spotty birdshit to tend our tamed pigeons and watch for my grandmother, who by now lived downstairs from Willa with a man named Jim that I called Fat Man. He returned the affection by calling me Fat Girl, but my curves didn't come from Willa's ketchup and bologna sandwiches, which I found as unappealing as I did her undignified mother.

We were arrested and sent to juvenile court. The boy faded into memory. Willa wisely turned down the invitation to live with the probation officer. I reported to the probation office every week, where I sat in a paper-filled stark office and listened to Mrs. Harvey lecture me about being a credit to my race. It wasn't long before I was staying out all night in alcohol blackouts, waking in the morning with the thick tongue, grinding headache, and brooding stomach that I came to associate with having had a good time.

At fourteen I was sent to Haines House. My earlier years in Aunt Erm's garden gave me the opportunity for outside chores; my ineptitude at serving made me self-conscious and clumsy at the table when it was my turn to pour coffee into the pastor's raised cup. Above all, my inexperience with discipline sent me daily to the pastor's office, where he forced me to kneel at a wooden chair while he loudly prayed for the salvation of my unwashed soul. After the session it was time for dinner, when I was again called on to demonstrate my salvation by seeing to the needs of the pastor and his wife, pouring coffee, serving cutlets, washing plates. A few weeks later, a twenty-one-year-old white boy from Juneau showed up at the gate with a big car and bigger plans.

We were arrested in Idaho. After days of detention in Idaho, again in Washington State, and then in Juneau, I was sent to a missionary boarding school in Valdez, where I spent the winter taking my turns mopping floors and washing dishes, often sent to the pastor's office to kneel while he exhorted me to contemplate the wide road upon which I seemed now to be traveling. I was sent back to Juneau the following summer, where my mother threw her hands in the air in a spirit of determined surrender while I wildly tried the town's patience. The following year, she moved to California and I went along. It wasn't long before we went our separate ways, she to an isolated life of relief and quiet interests, and I to a life of wandering in a dark forest called California.

By my grandmother's stories and by my own adventures I came to know the land upon which I was placed by birth. Later in life I spent many years in California, but I never forgot my home. Finally I returned belatedly to pursue a modern education. To finance my education, I worked at summer jobs in which I entertained and educated tourists. To give them better understanding, I learned new things about our ancient lands. I learned new stories to weave with the old.

At seventeen million acres, the Tongass National Forest is the largest national forest in the United States, part of the largest intact temperate rainforest in the world. Many names for the region have risen over the two hundred and fifty years since first European contact. Nowadays it is commonly called Southeastern Alaska to distinguish it from the rest of the state. Some people call it the Panhandle, others the Alexander Archipelago. Within the state, most people refer to it simply as Southeast. But there was a time when all the land from south of Prince of Wales Island northward to beyond Yakutat and Icy Bay was known as Lingít Aaní. The land of the people.

The land now known as Southeast Alaska is rich. Five kinds of salmon come to our shores: humpback, coho, chinook, sockeye, chum. Many fish live in our waters: halibut, cod, herring, eulachon, rockfish, trout. Fish to eat fresh, fish to dry for winter, fish to smoke. And not just the flesh of the fish. Place hemlock branches beneath the water when the herring are on their way (Sitka is the best place to do this). After the herring have spawned, pull up the branches covered with herring eggs for a traditional delicacy. In Juneau, when it's time for the herring to spawn, we wait for news that herring eggs have arrived from Sitka. We get word that eggs are being given away at the tribal building, or a message that down at the harbor a fishing boat is giving away branches. Even those of us who no longer have big families can still share, can smell on the gathered eggs the sea from which they were pulled, can relish the fresh spring flavor and hear the crunch of tiny eggs as they pop inside our happy mouths, seal grease dripping from our grateful hands.

And not just fish from the waters. Seaweed of more than one type, to collect in the spring, to dry and to use throughout the year in cooking —it's best when cooked with salmon eggs—or to eat dry like popcorn. Clams, cockles, king crab, Dungeness. Gumboots, sea urchin, mussels. Shrimp. Abalone. Seals for seal meat and seal grease.

And not just the waters. From the forest, all kinds of berries. Salmonberry, huckleberry, blueberry, raspberry, soapberry, cranberry, nagoonberry, Jacob berry, strawberry, thimbleberry—every berry that can be imagined, to eat fresh, to dry, to preserve in seal oil for a taste of summer during the darkened winter night. Wild celery, wild lettuce, wild rhubarb. Greens and herbs of all sorts. Birds for their eggs, especially seagulls. Deer meat. Mountain goat. Porcupine. Bears for their hides. Wood from the thick forest. Cedar for carving, spruce for making into our houses, hemlock for burning in our fires. It is a rich land indeed, our Lingít Aaní, our land of the people. Our ancestors' land.

Some people like to say that it is because the land is so rich that we developed the elaborate social system and sophisticated art forms for which our people are known—yellow cedar carvings, red cedar bentwood boxes and house screens, stylized woven blankets, formline painting and design.

It is true that ours is one of the most intricate art forms in the world, with difficult conventions, delicate techniques. And certainly our culture is complex. Upon the land that is now Southeast Alaska, we—the original people, the Lingít—developed a matrilineal society with a richness of culture rivaled only by the richness of our ancestral land. We take from the land our history and our stories, we identify our clans with our cousin the brown bear and our ancestor the raven, we honor the fish upon which we depend by taking them as crests. Ours is not a history that could have taken place anywhere. It is a history that could have been realized only upon the very land from which our culture receives its essential spirit.

The Lingít nation, the whole group of people united by common physical boundaries, language, and by custom, is the first order of social classification: the people who live on Lingít Aaní are one people. Next is the division into two subgroups, the Eagle and the Raven. Contemporary scholars call these two groups moieties, but my grandmother only ever called them sides. Sometimes the Eagle side is also called the Wolf side, perhaps taken from one of its largest clans, now called the Wolf clan, but who once had as their main crest the Eagle. Nevertheless, there are only two sides. The two sides occupy a ceremonial reciprocal relationship to one another and sustain the balance that is fundamental to the Lingít worldview. Traditionally, an Eagle marries a Raven. When Raven ears are pierced, it is by tradition an Eagle who takes up the ceremonial needle. When an Eagle wants a new pole or screen or bentwood box, by tradition he commissions a Raven carver to choose the wood, to make the design, to cut the cedar. When a Raven dies, it is the Eagle who acts as pallbearer, who sees to the business of death, who comforts Raven relatives in their grief, who wipes away Raven tears from beloved Raven faces.

Next comes the clan. The clan forms the basic political unit; it is the clan with which an individual most profoundly identifies; it is the clan to which one's allegiance is owed. It is the clan that forms relationships. The clan owns the crests, the stories, the histories, the right to use different parts of the land. And the names. We do not own our names. The clan owns our names. It is the clan that must never be denied and must never be abandoned. It is the clan that will live on.

Next, the house groups, made up of related individuals in a matriline. Sometimes house groups become so large that they split off; they occasionally become new clans if they are large enough, powerful enough, rich enough. Sometimes clans separate for other reasons: envy, jealousy, rivalry over a woman. A woman's word. A woman's glance. Sometimes such a thing divides the clan; when one group leaves, it might become a new clan. Then there will be another clan upon the face of Lingít Aaní. This is one of the ways in which the culture is meant to remain alive.

But old thoughts have been replaced by new. Old traditions have been forgotten. In the old way, women were known to be powerful. Then a new way of thinking was adopted that made it fashionable to look upon women as inferior, weak, dirty. In the old way, women had equal word — often the last word. Then a new way of thinking was adopted that gave them no word at all. In the old way, a woman's glance could petrify a man. Now it is taught that the old ways were carried out for other reasons. Now the christian thought that women are unclean has been laid upon an old respectful custom. Now it is taught that girls once were put behind a screen upon menarche because they were polluted. Now it is taught that women were not to mingle with men or step into fresh water while her moon was upon her because her blood was offensive. But that is a kind of reasoning thought up by people from an ungenerous desert forced to placate a god who became angry when he saw his children naked.

In the old Lingít way of thinking, a woman's blood exemplifies her power. A girl upon menarche must sit seed until she learns how to control all this authority that is suddenly upon her. She must contemplate her new power. She must not rejoin the rest of the community until she has learned how to control her glances and her words, for she is so powerful that one glance from her will turn a man to stone. One word from her will break a clan.

There was a young girl of the Chookeneidí, a powerful clan. Her family put her behind a curtain at the beginning of her enrichment, where she was isolated until she could use her powers well. She stayed there by herself in an extension of the house; she was not to look at the sky, she could not glance at men. She was to wait and learn to use her power well. As soon as her isolation was completed, she would be married.

This girl's time was almost finished, and soon she would be married. Because this girl was high class, she stayed a little longer behind the curtain. Her words held more power because of her station. Because she was high class, she needed more time to learn how to use her power well.

All the houses sat at a large place where grass grew on clay soil. Glaciers were within sight. From where this girl sat at the back of the house, she could see a glacier in the distance.

Her mother sent dryfish to her by the younger sister. The girl behind the screen ate almost all of it, until what was left was no more than a bony piece. She spit on the bones. She spit on what was left of her food as one spits on food for a dog. She reached under the curtain and began calling the glacier in the manner that one calls a dog. "Here glacier, here glacier. Haagú," she might have said. That was not a good thing, to call a glacier like a dog. It was not a good thing to speak to the glacier at all.

The girl's younger sister saw her do this. The younger sister, the little girl, ran to the front of the house and told her mother that her sister had called the glacier with sockeye dryfish. "Here glacier, here glacier. Haagú," she might have repeated to her mother. But her mother told the younger daughter not to speak of such a thing.

Not long later, the people of the village noticed that the glacier was advancing. It was growing. It was growing from the bottom and advancing, and no one knew why. People gathered together and asked themselves, "Why is the glacier doing this?" Almost like a dog the glacier ran. It made large noises and moved the water in strange ways.

But the girl's mother knew why the glacier acted in this way. She told the people that her daughter had called to the glacier and had teased it. It was then that the people knew they must prepare in their minds a place to go. They knew then that they must picture in their minds a place to go and they must go there.

The girl who called the glacier felt that she must stay. But her place was taken by her grandmother. My granddaughter is still a young woman, the grandmother must have said. She will have children, and I expect to die. I will take her place.

The people packed food and belongings into their boats. The whole village prepared to leave. There was hardly any time to prepare. The people were frightened because the glacier came so fast. The sounds it made were loud all over the land. It was like white thunder all over the land. The water churned in the bay from the glacier moving fast, like an earthquake.

The people did not leave their homes without grief. They knew the land would grieve for them. They knew the land would miss them.

Some of the people from that time went to other places. Their histories diverged, and they became new clans. The people of the Burnt House of this Chookeneidí village went to a place near Ground Hog Bay. They grew large and powerful and became a new clan. But the Burnt House people count in their history the day that Chookeneidí girl called a glacier to that village.

Most of the people went to a place close to the ice, where they could look toward their beloved home. A place where they could watch, always looking in the direction of that grassy place at the top of the bay, always waiting for the time when they could go back to their home. But when the ice decided to make room for them again, when the ice moved back and made room for them to come home, white people had taken their home away and had turned it into a national park and had named it Glacier Bay. The Chookeneidí people were forbidden to go home. They were told to stay at the place where they had gone. They live there still. They live there still, where they can watch their home, always looking in the direction of that grassy place at the top of the bay, always waiting for the time when they can go home.

When Chookeneidí people speak of their home, their eyes and their hearts turn always toward that place. When they talk about their home, they agree with the man who said, looking over to the shores where the ice once was, "I can't help but place my love there."

After we moved to California, I took over the kitchen, teaching myself from a bible titled *The Joy of Cooking*. I studied the descriptive passages and explanations, I memorized the correct approach to setting and serving, as well as the proper selection and preparation of food. I worked my way through admonitions on platter presentation and tips on napkin folding. Reading about cloth napkins and the presentation of entrees made my stomach hurt. In restaurants, I could neither order nor eat. But I taught myself to cook, and when I discovered plain, commonsense recipes, I taught myself to cook dishes that were closest to my memories of Aunt Erm's table.

As a child, I'd been sent to Aunt Erm's when my grandmother's house was in uproar, and Aunt Erm's food meant safety to me. I had worked in her garden and played with her dog; a garden and a dog now meant an orderly home life. Later, I served my own children garden-fresh vegetables and fruits from the orchard, organically raised beef, homemade granola, and sage-flavored honey. The memories of Aunt Erm's food were part of who I became, and in re-creating her cooking it became part of my children's memories. She was part of who they became. They didn't know her, but she contributed to their memories.

Years later, when I returned to my birthplace, I coveted the Native food of my childhood. I wanted to learn how to dry seaweed. A friend and I drove out to the beach and gathered it. I had been told by friends down at the Arctic Bar that all I had to do was spread the seaweed in the sun, turn it now and then, and salt it if I chose.

It was a cloudy day. I had read that I could dry the seaweed in a clothes dryer as long as I put the wet seaweed in a clean pillowcase and set the dryer on its coolest air fluff setting. I couldn't find a clean pillowcase, but I found a clean sheet. I tied the seaweed into the sheet and set the timer for one hour, already proud of my seaweed. After a couple of beers, I checked the seaweed. When I opened the dryer door I found that the sheet had come untied. Countless specks of green seaweed caked the drum. I spent hours scraping and cleaning the dryer, and after that attempt, all my seaweed was bought or bartered.

My friend decided he'd put up what he called Aleut-style dryfish. The method, he explained, was simply to cut the fish in two strips and hang it raw in the living room. I mistrusted this recipe, but he assured me it would work. By the second day, the stinking fish hanging at the door was crawling with flies. I walked down to the bar to demand that he get rid of the rotting fish. After a few beers, we walked back up the hill and threw the fish down the hill into the grass-covered field. From then on, I bought salmon jerky at the grocery store and pretended it was dryfish.

I miss the food of my childhood. I can neither gather nor prepare those old Native staples. I miss my grandmother's voice. I can't hold a conversation in my Native language. Illegitimate and fatherless, I live at the edge of the village. Nonwhite and unpolished, I live on the fringes of town. I wander down the aisles of my childhood searching for gumboots and berries. I fill my basket with sugar and bread and carry it home, where I sit alone in my room, hungry for dryfish.

Tom's baby was due to be born at the end of the season. He hoped for a boy. If it turned out to be a boy, he'd name the child Tom, after himself. Tom Junior. A modern name. His wife, Louise, hadn't wanted him to leave on this trip; she was due any day and afraid to be alone, but Susie, still their neighbor, was also expecting a child, would give birth somewhere around the same time, and was even more of a friend to Louise than she was to Tom. They needed the money, and the truth was that Tom didn't feel like a full man unless he was out on the water. So he left her with the promise he'd be back with money at the end of the summer's last trip and patted her tight, round stomach, feeling for the strong kick of a good lively son. He kissed the top of her head, rubbed her belly, and left. That was two months before.

They were on their way home now with a last load of salmon in the fish hole, anxious to sell the fish and be off the boat for a while. Being on the water was the same as ever, the water wouldn't change. Fishing boats and captains and regulations and even the fish might change, but the smell of the ocean, the feel of the spray, the sound of the gulls, the taste of the salt, the sight of mountain behind mountain behind island behind island falling back and back in shadows and gray and dark green would never change.

Let us look to Lingít Aaní. On the surface of the forest floor are fresh needles and twigs. Just beneath this, fallen berries and cones. On the damp ground, rotting, cool, shaded, rich, soft almost-earth. Then the substance of seasons gone, the generations of rot: decayed totems, grandfather's bones, spilled juices flavor and nurture and enliven, together with the rain. The deeper the darker the richer the more and more silent, more and more real/truth/is. In its essence, the light and the sky, the soft, clear drops of sweet heavenly nectar of the clouds: rain. Dripping from the berry bushes, the light of the whole day captured and intense in the corner of the sparkle in the drop just now falling from the sky, just now erupting onto the forest floor, nurturing, flavoring, bringing with it the whisper of what binds us. Surely on this water planet — in this ocean cosmos — this rainy day, this rain forest on this water planet — this is the natural order at its highest. Look to the forest. Look to Lingít Aaní.

Ice on the flats is melting. Dusk and dawn grow longer, so does the day. Only the night seems shorter, but midnight seems just as dark. Only the night is still. On the water are reflections we cannot explain. Perhaps they are the trapped spirits of those who have died there.

People who drown come back to life as Kóoshdaa Káa. They can be heard just outside our houses. As soon as we sense their soundless movement, they make themselves sound like bushes scraping on the wood and other such things. They might be seen anywhere. They can look like any ordinary thing, often people in our families or others whom we know. We have no reason not to trust them. If we go with them we will probably not come back right away. When we do come back, our loved ones will avoid us.

Behind the southeast wind the voice of the earth is singing. I lie alone in the sunset hoping to hear. Heat and the breeze soothe me and I am lost forever in the moment until a distant sound startles and I am wide awake, listening. But the sound becomes an eagle, or the creek, or a woman's wail. Once again I slumber. Once again I dream.

I am walking through an autumn evening fair in San Francisco. The plaza is full of benches and tables of treasure and food. It's not quite time to open; vendors are checking their wares. They arrange onions and incense, raw fish and beads. Children run. Young men throw Frisbees. Old men snooze. Laughter and shouts, snores and voices, all become one. Buildings stitch themselves into patchwork on the streets. Grey concrete walls, redletter billboards. Halfhearted neon. The far side of the plaza sports fountains and gulls. Everything sings. I am part of the song.

I wake into ribbons of sunlighted berries and then into the night. I hear a woman's cry. Her wail becomes the song. In the morning I do not remember my dreams.

Summer changes to winter. The long month approaches. Fish lie dead in the stream. Days become shorter. The dark months whisper soft, early calls, pushing clouds and wind before them, warning all who have not yet returned to winter camp: go home. Soon there will be snow on the mountains.

Many summers come again and so do many winters; my life goes on. I come to myself in San Francisco, forty years old and my life in shambles. Alone. Broke. Determined to go back home or to die facing north.

When Tom got back to Juneau, he signed on with the *St. Patrick*, one of the few seine boats owned and run by Natives. He hadn't made as much money that first year as he'd hoped, but he was glad to be back on any boat at all and felt lucky to be accepted late in the season. The way they divided the shares was unfair; the captain took a share, his son, who did almost nothing, took a share, and the boat got half a share. They took out half a share for the captain's wife, whom everyone called The Admiral, and who most of the time didn't even come along. The only thing worse than The Admiral taking a share without being on the boat was The Admiral being on the boat, so nobody complained too much about her share.

On top of all that, they were stingy with food. They didn't fully stock the galley until right before the last trip, when they went to all the stores and bought lots of everything. At the end of the season, the captain took all the extra food to his own home, charging the crew for all the supplies and food whether they ate it or not. During the rest of the trips, they ate twice a day and any snacks in between had to be either a peanut butter sandwich or a jelly sandwich. Sometimes the captain stopped the boat and sent a couple of men in the skiff to shoot a seal. On those times, the captain allowed the crew to eat a meal of seal meat, along with the bycatch of rockfish, salmon, and sometimes halibut, the always-present pot of rice, and maybe some canned peas. In the morning they had strong coffee and mush. It wasn't a bad life.

Tom knew the captain would make him wait as long as he could to cash out. It didn't matter to the captain or The Admiral if there were bills, a new baby, a reason to want to be happy. But Tom would be happy anyway if Louise was fine. If the baby was fine. After finishing as much work as the captain could force, Tom left the boat carrying a gunnysack full of fish and seal meat and some canned goods he'd hidden away during the trip. It was enough to tide them over until the captain let go of his share.

He rushed home. Letting himself inside, he smelled a baby at once. Quietly he walked to their bedroom off the kitchen, listening for any sound. As he approached, he heard the grumble of a baby at the breast.

The first time he'd gone downtown with Susie on a Saturday night, there in a bar named Dreamland he'd seen Louise in the middle of the dance floor, fancy-stepping by herself to a big-band jukebox tune. He was dazzled by her jitterbug and by her flirty ways. He didn't even want any beer; if he started drinking he'd drink too much and would probably wake up wondering where he was and where Louise was. So he drank soda water and watched Louise and Susie dance and flirt, and he waited. He bought them beer and tried to dance to the popular sounds of Glenn Miller.

But Louise and Susie both paid too much attention to other men, especially the few military men still in town. Tom waited. He waited two weekends and then three, taking a janitor job at the newspaper building so most of his winter hours were free and his Saturday nights were open. Finally after a month, Louise gave in and said he could walk her home. It was cold, almost the modern holiday known as Thanksgiving. Sideways snow and the Taku Wind forced Louise to huddle against Tom and hold on to his arm, which he kept diligently flexed for the whole half-mile walk to the village, hoping she'd be overcome by the firmness of his muscles. Louise lived in the village with her aunt a few doors down the dirt street from Susie. She didn't like living with her aunt, she said. She was nothing more than babysitter and cook. She couldn't wait to be married and leave, start her own family. Tom steered her toward his house, saying she could come in for a beer. He carried a bottle in his pocket and with it he enticed her to his front door. When he promised to put wood on the fire in the kitchen, she gave in.

He still hadn't been with a woman since San Francisco. For a while he had dreamed of Susie, but her big-sister ways discouraged him, and after a while he asked her to introduce him to her friends. When she relented and took him to meet Louise, he vowed to himself that he would always be grateful.

Tom thought he was in love from the very first moment, but he didn't know what love was until Louise allowed him into her pants. There, in the curtained-off kitchen on a cot pushed against the far wall, she laid back and carefully set the empty beer bottle on the floor at the edge of the bed. "I'm sleepy," she sighed, and rested her head on the flat uncovered pillow. She closed her eyes and sighed again.

Tom didn't know what to do but he knew not to waste time doing nothing. Quickly he sat beside her, slipping his shoes off, hoping his feet didn't stink. He leaned his face toward hers and tasted her lips with his tongue. He placed a hand under her head and lifted her face closer to his so his tongue entered her mouth as he drew her closer. He placed his other hand on her breast over her blouse. It was soft. It was firm. It was water swirling at the base of a waterfall, and as Tom sank beneath the rushing and roaring of her lips and the skin beneath her blouse, he knew that this was love.

On the modern holiday Christmas, he bought her a pink-tinted nylon blouse and a bottle of Emeraude perfume. Since that first time a month before, she'd gotten in bed with him just about every time he wanted, which was pretty much every time he saw her alone. Tom was almost twenty-one, Louise a couple of years older. He couldn't keep his mind off her when they weren't together; he couldn't keep his hands off her when they were. He watched her unwrap her presents, sitting on the cot that had become Tom's favorite place in the world. He pulled her to him.

"Stop!" she laughed. "Let me see my present!"

Tom watched her pick the ribbons off the two presents. She was still dressed in her waitress clothes, new dress-up black Christmas slacks carelessly draping her hips, cotton blouse half tucked.

"Mmmm." She tore open the package. "Emeraude." She opened the bottle and smeared a drop on each wrist, dabbed a sprinkle behind each ear. "Smell me." She leaned toward him and nuzzled her head on his chest.

"Try on your blouse," he whispered in her perfumed ear. "Let me see you try it on."

"Naughty!" she laughed. She began to unbutton her shirt.

Tom unbuttoned her shirt from the bottom. When they met in the middle, he opened her old shirt and slipped it off her shoulders. He stopped her when she started to put on her new blouse. "Take this off," he said, pulling at her brassiere.

She looked surprised at first, but then smiled. "You do it," she whispered.

When it was off, he looked at her, forcing himself not to touch her. "Now put this on," he whispered, handing her the blouse. He dressed her like a doll and helped her button two buttons in the front. "That's enough," he said.

He unzipped her dark slacks and pulled them off her legs along with the rest of her clothes. She lay back on his cot in the warm kitchen, dressed in a see-through pink nylon blouse with only two buttons fastened, and ran her hands along the inside of her thighs, looking at him. "Come love me," she said. He would never have enough of her. He would love her forever. He would want her always.

Three months later they were quickly married by the Presbyterian preacher, with Susie and a couple of his friends as witnesses. Louise's aunt refused to come to the wedding, and Tom had no family left to invite. Louise had gotten all her wishes; she was moving out of her aunt's house, getting married, and starting a family all at the same time. She was happy and Tom was dazed. Dazed but no longer dazzled.

At sunset the salmon wait at the waters in great numbers. Even the waters far inland, the waters at the end of the longest journey, receive the salmon again like a mother greets that child who wandered the farthest away from her and who stayed away for the longest time. The salmon children who came back to the streams and lakes farthest inland fought the hardest to reach their homes. The waterfalls over which they jumped, the bears, the eagles, the gulls, the people lining the shores as glad for their return as were the salmon themselves, none of that stopped these triumphant many who have finally come back to the place where they first quickened, the place where they were buried in their mother's gravel, the place where the bodies of their mothers and fathers nourish the ground. But even these salmon will die when they have accomplished their purpose. Even these salmon will swim away to die.

The bear feels fat. It was a good summer. Her two cubs are playful, and their bellies are full of salmon. They have come to a favorite inland lake to feast even more than they feasted in the summer at their first glimpse of the salmon's return. Here at the lake, life is easier. Bears are fatter. Everyone has been eating for some time, so the danger of fighting to protect their catch is lessened. Everyone is pleasantly full. Most of the salmon they will store for winter has already been gathered. It won't be long before it is time for the bear to turn her nose toward higher ground.

When the salmon have diminished, she and her cubs will leave. When her dripping mouth no longer waters at the thought of brains and fat, she will leave. When there are few eggs left in fewer fish in water stinking with the death of life, she will leave. She and her cubs will turn toward the mountain. They will amble uphill through the willow. They will go farther and farther into the mountains, and they will play and rest along the way. They will eat berries and the end of the summer greens, putting a top on the summer's fat fish. They will investigate new and old places along the way and wonder at the deer and the moose they see here and there. They will make lazy efforts at catching a young deer or an old moose, or a ground squirrel surprised in the shade. An incautious field mouse. An unhatched egg in an abandoned nest. A few late berries caught napping.

Late in the fall they will begin their climb in earnest. When frost is in the air and the smell of snow tingles her nose, she will get busy. It's still a long way to the den. She must still prepare it. Make sure it's safe.

She feels sleepy. The crisp air reminds her there is a better place to be. This generation of salmon are all but dead. The next generation of salmon are buried in clusters in the gravel. The bear dreams only of sleep.

By fall, many of last year's salmon are beginning the journey that the others, now returning to spawn, are ending. The journey of this year's generation is toward salt water. No one knows exactly where they go; some salmon stay away for only a year, some for a longer time. By some force they are driven away from their mother streams, just as in a year or two years or more, they will be pulled back by an equally unexplained force. It is known only that they go. They go somewhere away from their home to grow, to mature, to learn, to wait that long long time before they finally respond to the irresistible call to return. The call away from home in the fall is as powerful and as important to their life cycle as that next call will be that brings them back to this place where they belong.

Many of the salmon now returning are caught by the people, using various means. Some salmon are caught in traps, some are taken on stakes. When the land was as it should be, there was enough for all the people, and all the bears, and all the eagles and gulls and ravens. Most important, there was enough for the salmon themselves to finish that cycle of life that guarantees that all our lives will be sustained and we will be rich. Fresh salmon is delicious, no one will deny it. Smoked salmon is a delicacy, no one will say any different. Fermented eggs, salted head, fish oil, all these are bounty from the salmon. But the staple of life, and the most delicious, is the salmon's dried flesh. Dryfish. The best meal, the best snack, the best thing to take with you when you travel.

When you carry the fish you have just caught, make sure you never let it touch the ground. Especially do not drag it. When you put it down, make sure its head always faces upriver, the direction it is meant to go, the direction its spirit will always desire. Cut the fish from belly to throat. Clean out the insides. Cut off the salmon head, place it with the others — it will be good to boil or to bury for a while and allow to ferment. Or you can dry the heads separately, and the tails separately. Or you can get the oil out of them, oil to flavor next winter's comforting meals.

For the dryfish, cut out the backbone and cut the salmon flesh again, opening it like a bird's wings or like the stingray in the water. After you cut it like this, if it's big enough you can cut it again and even again— thin is good. Then, split in that manner, hang it on your drying racks placed where flies don't want to go, near some good smoke. Let the fish dry. Watch it carefully. Make sure it's just right.

When you have plenty of dryfish you don't have to worry about what you're going to eat. Dryfish is always good. Hand it to children to nibble on. Let your old grandmother suck on it; the edges get soft and never lose their flavor, even if it takes her all day to work on it. Grab off a good piece for your own snack, lick it and sprinkle some salt. Dip it in seal oil. Soak it in water. Toss some dried flakes into the soup. You are rich when you have plenty of dryfish. You will never have to worry about what to offer your guests. When you have dryfish you will never go hungry. When you have dryfish things will always be good.

In the unlit room, Tom couldn't make out the bed or the window, or whether clothes and dishes were still scattered on the floor the way they were in the weeks before he jumped thankfully onto the *St. Patrick* and lit out for deep water. But Louise's face and uncovered breasts seemed to glow; Tom could make out a little face at her dark, large nipple. "Is it a boy?" he whispered, standing perfectly still.

"Yes," she answered. "A boy. Tom Junior." A modern name.

He didn't want his boy to be called Junior or Little Tom, so they started calling the baby Young Tom. This led to his being called Old Tom. Young Tom and Old Tom. Friends and neighbors laughed at calling Tom, who was now all of twenty-two, Old Tom. But in only a year, he felt like he'd already grown into his new name.

Louise never recovered from giving birth. Her skin was drawn, her cheeks sunken where they should be fat. Her energy was low all the time and she wept, sometimes for days. Tom took over more and more of the chores, coming home in the winter from his janitor job and cleaning the baby, cooking, gathering wood for the dwindling fire, bringing Louise water or soup or a magazine, trying to cheer her and take care of the boy and the house. In the summer, he gladly got back on the *St. Patrick*.

Susie, who'd given birth to a baby girl she named Nadine a month before Young Tom was born, moved in and took care of Louise and both babies and the house and cooking and cleaning when she was home from her more than fulltime job in the tuberculosis ward at the Indian hospital. While she was at work, she arranged for two or three of her friends to take turns dropping by to change diapers and spoon cereal into waiting baby mouths. Susie kept working and Louise continued to fail.

During the second year, Louise rallied for the summer, but as soon as Tom came off the boat she collapsed into the bed again and stayed there. Susie now lived with them full time. It took all of Old Tom's and Susie's energy and time to take care of the children. Together they were able to pay bills and buy enough groceries, taking turns cooking and cleaning. Old Tom knew that Susie was saving money for herself, but he was glad she helped at all. He knew it was a hardship on her, and he admired her for the way she insisted on paying her own way.

More than once Old Tom had come home from work to find Susie cradling Louise's head on her lap, stroking her forehead while Louise wept, the children playing in the kitchen on the barewood floor, a fire warming the house, a pot of stew on the stove, the house clean and Louise weeping, her sobs and sighs muffled by her friend's caring belly. Louise wouldn't talk to Tom. Her skin burned him when he touched it.

Louise hadn't cried for days, and Old Tom was thinking she might be getting better. But Susie was concerned. "Louise," she whispered each morning. "Louise, wake up, come with me to the hospital, get up and come see the doctor." Susie fed the children and put the dishes to soak. "Louise," she tried again. "Louise, try to get up." Susie gently shook her friend's shoulder. She made sure the doors and windows were secured so the children couldn't get out, placed some pilot bread and hardtack on the table for them to help themselves to later on, and quietly closed the door. The last thing she glanced at before she walked out the door was Louise on the cot, one dry hand covering her mouth, the children sitting on the floor in the early summer sunlight catching dust motes in the air with pudgy fingers.

In the spring of the year that the babies turned four years old, Louise turned her face to the wall and died. Old Tom was stunned. He'd always thought that she'd get better, they'd both become young and laugh and jitterbug again. He'd always had it in the back of his mind that one night he'd come home and she'd be sitting on the cot, Young Tom asleep and the rest of the house somehow empty. She'd be dressed in a pink nylon blouse with only two buttons fastened, and she'd call his name and motion for him to love her, and things would get better right away.

He started drinking again. Susie took care of both children, and kicked Old Tom out of the house whenever he came home drunk. She enrolled both children in school, and helped them with their homework, and sent away to the catalog for their clothes, and took them out picking berries and fishing and gathering seaweed and wild celery. She took all of Tom's money whenever she caught him and kept the house clean and warm. When the children were ten years old, she enrolled herself in the business school in Tacoma, and offered to take Young Tom. But the BIA wouldn't pay for it, and her asking for permission made them curious, and as soon as Susie and Nadine left for Tacoma the social workers began keeping their eye on Old Tom and the boy. It was only a few months before they took Young Tom.

Young Tom was ten when they took him away, the same age as Old Tom had been when they'd taken him away. They took Young Tom to the same place they'd taken Old Tom years ago, to the missionary school up in Haines. Old Tom sent his son money now and then, but he never tried to visit.

Young Tom came back to Juneau when he was nineteen. He'd tried to enlist in the army, but they wouldn't take him because they said there was something wrong with his ears. Old Tom was still fishing, still drinking, still living in the old house. When Young Tom signed on to the *St. Patrick*, Old Tom just stayed in town instead of going fishing. The next year, Young Tom married a girl named Lucille and they had a baby right off the bat, a little girl they named Patricia.

With Young Tom on his own, Old Tom was the only one who lived in the old house. In a few years, the city people tore it down. They said the old house was a hazard. After that, Old Tom slept in cars abandoned on the property and ate at the new food line they'd started on South Franklin

Street, using his sporadic Indian money for drinking, keeping the cash in an envelope in a post office box at the new federal building built where the Indian hospital used to be. It wasn't long before he noticed Young Tom's little girl, Patricia, coming around and drinking. She couldn't have been more than twelve or thirteen years old.

When Nadine and Susie finally came back to Juneau, Nadine remembered him, calling him Uncle Old Tom and giving him money when she could, but Susie pretended she didn't recognize him.

Just as well, Old Tom thought. By then, he'd lost whole chunks of his life to the numbing blackouts that came every time he drank. He'd cash a dividend check and start drinking, secretly buying bottles of vodka, pop, and wine, sipping and gulping while sitting alone in some abandoned car on the old property in the village. Before long, he'd be humming and crooning to himself and singing and weeping and talking out loud to his lost mother, his bent father who had never come back. Days and sometimes weeks went by while he stayed in cars and drank. Patricia and others occasionally came by to help him drink; people like his son's friend Norman brought him food, which he wolfed down and never remembered eating. One morning he'd wake up, clothes stiff with dried piss, crushed paper bags and empty bottles scattered everywhere, his stomach burning and his throat tasting like puke. Outside the rusted car, dandelion puffs floating in a beam of sunshine would remind him of healthy days and a mother's love, and he'd check himself into the recovery house, where nurses and social workers cleaned him up and weaned him slowly from the bottle.

A few months after Susie and Nadine came back to town, Old Tom went on a bender, and when he woke up he learned that Young Tom had fallen off a boat over by Hoonah and drowned. He sobered up in time to make it to the funeral. By then Old Tom's brain was so far gone he thought Young Tom's death was something that had happened to him, nothing more than a speck of memory drifting in the shadowed sunlight. He knew he was lost. He wondered if Young Tom had forgotten or remembered him in the moments before he died. He sometimes talked about buying a headstone for his dead son's unmarked grave, but after a while it became just one more thing to cry about when he was drunk.

Richard King Sr., my maternal grandfather, of the Gunáx teidí clan, and Susie James King, my maternal grandmother and namesake, in Klukwan, Alaska, circa 1900.

Uncles Albert "Skip" Hayes (seated) and Ernest "Buzz" Hayes (far right) in front of the Pioneers' Home in Sitka, Alaska, not far from Sheldon Jackson College, circa 1940s.

Note: All photographs are from the family collection. The older photographs are from the collection of Erma Daisy Hayes, deceased.

My mother, Erma Daisy
Hayes, with me in 1946.

to mom

Love
Ernie

Here I am at the beach
at Aunt Erm's house on
Douglas Island across from
Juneau in 1950. The photo
is inscribed to my mother,
who was then hospitalized
in the Seward tuberculosis
sanitorium.

In this photo I'm standing at the edge of the Juneau Indian village, circa 1949.

Here I am about two years later in the doorway of our old house in the Juneau Indian village.

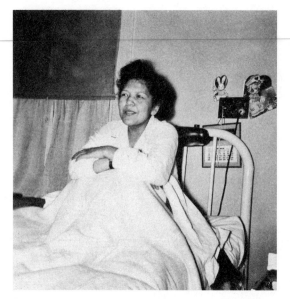

My mother while she
was hospitalized in the
Seward tuberculosis
sanitorium in 1950.

The Native hospital in Juneau, Alaska, where I was born and where my
mother was hospitalized during early stages of tuberculosis, circa 1950.

Here I am at the Juneau Indian village in 1951.

A family friend, James Manning ("Fat Man"), and me at the side of our old house in the Juneau Indian village, circa 1950.

Ruth Willard Hayes, my grandmother Saawdu.oo, and Ernest Leonard Hayes Sr., my grandfather, in 1948.

Ruth Willard Hayes and James Manning on South Franklin Street in Juneau in the 1950s.

Here I am with my mother in Roseville, California, circa 1974.

My mother and Gypsy in Ketchikan in 1988.

My mother with her great-grandson Rader in Juneau in 1992.

The Climax Forest

Once there was a man who lived in a large town. Although the man was born to a woman of high status, his father was not from the original people. Because of that, his childhood was awkward. As he grew, it became impossible for his mother to control him. His father also was unable to manage him. His maternal uncle, the one who should have taken over the boy's upbringing, wanted nothing to do with him. As a result, the boy grew into a wild and unhappy man.

The man, whose name was said by some to demonstrate nobility and by others to show his relation to the killer whale, was quick to combat and less quick to love. His loyalty and his ease with weapons were never questioned.

After many adventures on land and on water, and many loves of women and of girls, and many troubles on the hilltop as well as in his own home, there came a day when he looked out upon the waters where he sometimes fished, and at his apprehensive companions who were trying to cast off the fishing boat and head out to sea, and back at the land where they had cast anchor for the night, and he jumped off the boat and swam to the shallow part of the water and stood in the water and ran to the shore, with the salt water holding him back for as long as it could, and he ran onto the beach and into the woods, screaming unintelligible words at the top of his hoarse voice while his astounded crewmates could only stare at him and at each other dumbly until finally the captain gave them orders to drop anchor and man the skiff and they followed him to the edge of the forest, calling his name.

Over the years, my mother had told me little about my unknown father. When I was a young girl, she occasionally remarked that I had my father's chin. Taught never to challenge or question my elders, I received this extraordinary bit of information silently. I sat quiet and unmoving, trying with my thoughts to trace my chin. In bed, waiting for sleep while my mother played pinochle in the kitchen with my Uncle Buzz or my Aunt Pauline, I closed my eyes and felt my chin, re-creating it in my mind. To the image of my chin I added a jawline, square and perhaps with light brown whiskers to match the color of my hair and the rough scratch of Grandpa's face. I planted a straight, sharp nose in the middle, topped it off with brown eyes and curly hair to explain why my own hair curled when it got wet. I usually ended up with a mental picture of an Indian-fighting John Wayne or with the features of my Aunt Erm's white man husband Uncle George, he of cackleberry fame.

The other story she told me had taken place a few days after I was born. She had left me with my grandmother at our house in the village, she told me, and walked up Willoughby Avenue toward town. Ahead on the sidewalk she saw him. When they came close to one another, she asked him if he wanted to see me. He told her no.

Within my memory, my mother never kept company with another man. In the last few weeks of her life, she felt the presence of her grandparents standing by her bed and talked often of her childhood in their care. With thin dry fingers she plucked at smooth cool sheets I changed for her comfort every day. She recalled past feasts of grease-covered herring eggs spawned on branches and lifted from the rich salt water to be plucked from the hemlock, juices dripping, on this far future deathbed. Unseeing eyes searched above my head while she gazed at the memory of those brilliant young days. Sunshine. Bright paths full of berries. Patchwork forest high above the shadows. Dazzled by the sunlight, blinded eyes unseeing her distant old age. Gaunt whispers rasped her withered throat, echoing prayers and laughter, songs and sweet endearments to the child wrapped in her arms. Humming happy sleepy tunes, I bent near to receive her grieving words.

"Your father was the only man I ever loved."

After her death, I found a collection of old photographs, many of them featuring a wavy-haired smiling man. I searched the photos, examining his chin, his smile, his eyes, for traces of the man my mother had loved. I finally gave up and packed them all away. There was no way to know whether any of the men in the frayed old black-and-white pictures was the one for whom I searched. I could at last be sure, though, that it was no longer as important as once it had been. He may have been the only man my mother ever loved, but he was only the first of many who would never love me.

This is our story.

Young Tom had only a vague memory of his mom lying on a cot in the kitchen near the wall, the whisper of Auntie Susie recently disappeared like a shadow in sudden light, he and Nadine catching dust motes floating in a beam of sunshine from the bare window, wetting their pudgy fingers and sticking dust motes on one another's nose, digging into the pilot bread as soon as they realized they were alone except for his weeping mother, spreading crumbs all over the floor, children and crumbs unnoticed for hours. By the day Susie and Nadine left, the image of his mother came to him only in the moments before he fell asleep. He depended on Susie for his meals, for help with homework, for new clothes. He depended on Nadine for company and for someone to sleep near in a dark room. When Susie decided to leave, she sat Young Tom down and promised she'd send for him. But he and Nadine didn't realize how far they were going or how long they'd be away, and they ran outside to play kick-the-can with the other kids on Village Street until Susie called to Nadine and then they were gone.

That night his dad got drunk. "Get over here, boy," he called, and slammed an empty vodka bottle down on the wooden table. "Get over here." Young Tom was used to seeing his father slur and stagger on the docks or somewhere downtown. It wasn't unusual to see his dad drunk, but not in the house. Susie always made him leave when he was drinking. Young Tom stood near his father's shoulder and watched Old Tom's head slump until he thought his forehead would hit the table's edge. Old Tom's head snapped up and he focused on the boy. "Son," he said. His breath smelled like rotten grape syrup mixed with kerosene. "Sonny boy, now it's just you and me." He gave the boy a sloppy hug. Young Tom's arms were caught in the drunken vise of his father's still-strong grip. "It's just you and me, sonny boy," he said. "Just you and me."

Young Tom wriggled out of his father's hug and backed away a few steps. "Is there anything to eat?" he asked. Old Tom pressed his wet cheek on the smooth, cool table, still muttering. He didn't seem to hear his son's question.

Young Tom touched the rough, black lid of the soup pot with a careful finger. He lifted the smudgy lid and looked inside. The aroma of fish soup eased his worry. Chunks of potatoes and onions and pieces of fish floated in the liquid. Young Tom scooped a bowlful and sat at the table. He broke off some pilot bread, soaking it in the broth while he watched his father snore and drool.

Three months later a white lady dressed in a shiny grey skirt and an unfriendly jacket climbed out of a car and knocked on the door. Old Tom was passed out, snoring and stinking in the midmorning light. Young Tom hadn't been to school in at least two weeks, so he thought maybe a teacher had come to take him to school. He felt vaguely relieved; they were running out of food, and Mr. Stevenson kept asking about his father whenever he went into the market to charge crackers and candy. Young Tom opened the door and waited for her to speak.

Right before Susie and Nadine had left town, there'd been a big celebration for something everybody called Statehood. Before that, fireworks had been seen only on the Fourth of July, when waving pink women in fancy cars and clowns in bright feathered headdresses paraded on the street, and booths were set up at the submarine port where you could throw darts at balloons or fish for paper prizes, and at night the sky was filled with the odor of burnt powder and the flashes of booming flowers. The name of the current year's Fourth of July Princess, always a pink-toned Rainbow Girl from the Masonic Temple where neither Tom nor any of his neighbors or friends was expected ever to enter, would be lit up in a display of giant sparklers. Marilyn, it would say one year. Peggy, it spelled out on another year's evening.

Young Tom had watched the Statehood Fireworks and attended the Statehood Bonfire, running along with Nadine in front of Susie, who strolled behind them with her friend Erma. Old Tom was drinking down on the docks and later that night on South Franklin Street. Young Tom saw a white lady dressed in a shiny skirt and a jacket like this one now at the door. The lady had walked by them, holding back the hem of her jacket so she didn't touch Young Tom or Susie. Nadine had deliberately bumped Young Tom against the lady, and the lady had wiped her jacket like she'd been touched by something dirty. Maybe this was that same lady. Maybe she was here because of that night. Telling her that Nadine and Susie were now gone might calm her and make her go away. On the other hand, she might have boxes of groceries in her car such as ladies like her brought around right before Christmas.

"Tom Dan?" she said, smiling at him with bright red lips under rouged cheeks and pincurled hair.

"Young Tom," he corrected.

"Is your father home, Tom?" she asked. She held a flat purse, snapping and unsnapping the brass clasp with sparkling clean fingernails.

"He's asleep right now."

"May I come in, Tom?" Her voice was pliant, like the voices nurses at the Indian hospital used when they were going to stab a needle in his arm or press a dry Popsicle stick down his throat to make him gag. He wished she would stop saying his name.

"Young Tom," he corrected.

"Pardon me?"

"My name's Young Tom."

"May I come in and talk to your father?"

"He's asleep, I said."

She turned to a car parked on the side of the street and motioned with one hand. The doors opened and two men unfolded themselves from the doors. They were dressed in the funny brown suits that Young Tom saw on the principal at school and on other men walking from their cars into downtown buildings where Young Tom never went.

The two men approached Young Tom, smiling. "Hello, little fella," said the first one.

"He refuses to allow entrance," the lady said, her voice now clipped enough to betray her white lady irritation.

"Now let's just see about that!" the second man said in a loud false tone. He brushed past Young Tom and entered the front room. They all followed him and stood motionless just inside the door, listening to the sound of Old Tom's wet snores. One man stepped toward the sound, cocking his head like a dog when it hears an unlucky bird.

They hadn't managed to wake Old Tom that day. They let Young Tom pack a few things, some clothes, an old black-and-white picture of his mother and another of Nadine and Susie on the cold storage dock, Susie's head wrapped in a rolled scarf, Nadine holding a glass of soda, water and mountains and gulls in the background. They walked Young Tom to the car, each man holding an arm. The woman, Mrs. Keller she told Young Tom to call her, walked ahead, opening the car door, smiling, patting him, pushing him a little when he hesitated, tossing in the bent cardboard box of belongings he'd hurriedly collected. She scrunched in next to him on the back seat; the two men settled in the front. Mrs. Keller examined some papers, pulled a pen from her snapped purse, and wrote Tom's future in blue ink on designated lines.

They drove out of town toward the end of the road, farther than Young Tom had ever been. He began to worry if he should think about jumping out. He'd heard of people who liked to kill you, like that guy in the new movie the kids talked about, a crazy man who lived in a hotel on a road not unlike this one, who liked to stab women. Would these men try to stab him, maybe stab the woman first? Young Tom held the box of his belongings on his lap and watched for signs of danger.

"Now, Tom," Mrs. Keller began.

"Young Tom," he corrected.

"We're taking you to the ferry, and you'll board with Mr. Antrip, who will meet us at the terminal. You're going to a very nice place where you'll have plenty of food and the right upbringing. It's a wonderful, wonderful place. You'll receive the proper education there." Mrs. Keller smiled at Young Tom like she had a secret. "We know you haven't been attending school."

Young Tom said nothing.

When my mother and I first moved to San Francisco I wandered barefoot through Golden Gate Park, admiring the music of strumming guitars, throwing rice to the flocking pigeons, tasting the newness of generous drugs and free love. In North Beach I sat around Mike's Pool Hall sipping strong coffee and watching pretty people walk by on the crowded sidewalk. Standing on sands across the Little Great Highway not far from Seal Rocks, I fought the dizzying sight of an ocean unsoftened by mountains or islands or trees. I met a tall beautiful black man who called himself Sugar Ray; by the time he admitted that from his point of view I was just another white girl, I was pregnant. When he and I drifted apart, my mother invited me to live with her in an apartment on the other side of the Golden Gate Panhandle near Haight Street. I followed in my mother's footsteps and signed up for secretarial school. In short time, I had a new baby boy, a new job, and a new resolve to build a good home for my child.

Sitting with secretarial posture in the typing chair at the South of Market company where I worked, I had a clear view of the comings and goings of the delivery driver as he loaded custom springs into the pickup and hauled them out. He told me he was an Indian man from West Texas. I'd had no dealings in Alaska with people who claimed to be Native unless they actually were, and I had no reason not to believe him. Within a year, we were living together as a couple. Another year later, my second son was born.

With the end of the sixties, we signed up for the back-to-the-land movement and moved to the foothills of the Sierra Nevada, where I tended my gardens and gradually realized I was in a relationship with a man who had pretended to be Indian, had pretended to be patient, and had pretended to be peaceful. His anger grew more unreasonable as he placed us in isolated positions as caretakers on secluded properties. By the early seventies, I'd given birth to my third child, my spirit wept every day, and I sought relief from the violence of his spoken assaults in the back-to-jesus movement. I joined a holy ghost pentecostal church and prayed for a deliverance that would never come from overworked scriptures that counseled surrender and submission.

Sister Baglin's extralong hair modestly sways to her repetitious pounding on the upright piano in the corner. Dah duh duh dah, dah duh duh dah. Dah duh duh dah, dah duh duh dah. Her husband, sillygrin Brother Baglin, sits across the platform, strumming on his electric guitar, ready to put it down and jump on the drums, mouth harp strapped to his neck only a lipblow away. On the pulpit, at which he will begin a hellfire and brimstone holy ghost sermon guaranteed by the word of god to save souls as soon as he works up the crowd, sits the worn tambourine he taps on his elbows and knees when everything else is used up. Down in the audience, Sister Greene squints her whitelashed, pale blue godfearing eyes shut and whispers thank you jesus, while Sister Rauch, whose salvation is questionable only to those who question salvation, and to Brother Baglin, who is privy to her secrets, runs up and down the aisle turning the light switch at either end on, off, on, off, while she babbles in the unintelligible tongue of the truly anointed and gets ready to roll on the floor. Another good night praising jesus: praise the lord, thank you jesus, praise the lord.

I sit on a hard, polished pew with the baby in my lap, my two other children sitting quietly beside me. The man I live with perches stern and straight on the other side of the boys. I, too, am murmuring thank you jesus, waving my arm in the air every once in a while, wishing I could stand and shout and run up and down the aisle alongside Sister Rauch, whose salvation I privately question but whose unapologetic style I admire.

I wouldn't bother switching the lights on and off. Instead I'd run out the door, the baby still in my arms and my two children right behind me. We'd burst through the double doors and, while everyone sat waiting for us to run back in praising god, while everyone waved their arms high in the air shouting praise the lord, praise the lord, while all the saints, Sister Greene and Brother Baglin and Sister Baglin and Sister Rauch and Brother Greene and Sister Riley and her seven children and Sister Caroline in her silky dress and Brother Rauch with his smelly shoes and stained jacket and Brother Camrun with his swollen potbelly and bloated sense of self, while they all waited expectantly with the unsaved man I live with, rigid and unbending, sitting among them even more judgmental than they, sending everyone to hell as easily and as quickly as they do, with no more reason and no more mercy than they—my children and I would be running, flying, soaring out of this place on our way to somewhere free.

I'm backsliding. I've been at this jesus thing for a few years now, they call me Sister Ernestine, I teach Sunday school, I don't wear slacks or jewelry or makeup, I don't cut my hair or play card games or watch television or say gosh or darn. My two older sons are used to coming to this little country church four and five times a week; the baby is still nursing and sleeps at my breast through it all. After service on Sundays we drive home to a little house where there are two vegetable gardens and lots of flowers and a small orchard of fruit and olive trees.

I tend tomatoes and soak olives in lye and simmer pears and apples into sugary brown butter and I wait for salvation but it isn't coming from jesus. The man I live with is an asshole. If I were a stronger—or weaker?— woman I guess I'd kill him. I would rush out of the dry willows where he conceals himself. Seeing me, he would become afraid, but I would be on him. I would kill him. I would rip him to pieces.

But I stay with him because I don't know where to go or how I would take care of the children, and because I have made myself believe for these few years that if I pray and live a holy life, my prayers will be answered and I will be delivered. But Sunday school and bible study and the prayers of the saints have all let me down. Forcing myself to acquiesce to their intolerant, one-way damning of all others was doable only if I got in return the promised home life of peace and harmony. The man I live with, however, is no more susceptible to prayer than he is to reason. He will never be patient or kind or generous. He will always be the ill-tempered, mean-spirited, sneering asshole he'd revealed himself to be after I became pregnant, after our fates were locked. Now I suffer from ulcers that ache all the time, depression that makes me sit and stare, and hands that weep and bleed from blisters and dried sores cracked and oozing pus. He yells and curses every time any slight thing goes wrong and searches me out and berates me, for we are both convinced that I alone am to blame. And before I forget, thank you Jesus.

Keep believing, Brother Baglin tells me when I seek his advice. Stay with him. Even though this man and I are not married, for some reason Brother Baglin has identified us as man and wife, and so instructs me to stay, for the wife is to the husband as the church is to Christ. Or something like that. Never mind how mean he is, or what a tyrant. All that matters, I am told, is that he is the man and I am not. For the sake of the children, Brother Baglin says. For the sake of his soul, he says. For the sake of your own soul. This is what jesus wants you to do, Brother Baglin assures me, citing the word of god verse by memorized verse. So I suffer and endure, but slowly, irrevocably, inevitably, I backslide and dream of escape.

One day I will leave him, on my hands and knees but I will be free. I will leave my house, my children, my car, my clothes — but I will crawl away richer. I will lose all my possessions, he will slander me to my children, I will try to end my life after his stalking and threats and oppression and ugliness become too much for me. I will rise again from the flames of depression in a hot Nevada town and go through many many changes and wrongs and hard times and mistakes, but each time I find myself hungry and lonely and cold and sick I will remind myself that it could be worse: I could still be with him. At least, I will always tell myself, I'm not with that man anymore.

Haines House wasn't too bad. As soon as Young Tom learned to keep his uncomfortable clothes buttoned up to his neck even though he felt like he was choking, as soon as he knelt by the wooden chair at least five times every day, elbows on the seat, head bent, eyes squinted shut, face crumpled into an earnest frown as he listened to the preacher going on and on and on until Young Tom was dizzy and sweaty and hungry enough to eat even the thin unhappy vegetables grown in the outside gardens, boiled and stewed and mashed into dishes for lunches and dinners, as soon as he stopped trying to correct everyone who called him Tom instead of Young Tom, it wasn't too bad at Haines House.

He missed his dad, but not for long. Old Tom never tried to come see him, and Young Tom quickly learned the pleasures of clean sheets and plenty of food. A big bowl of vegetables and rice every day was more than he thought he could expect, and when the preacher's wife made something called cornbread and let him pour syrup on it, or fixed a new type of food she said was called tacos, stuffed with hamburger meat and chopped onion and lettuce fresh from the garden, he forgot all about being at home with Old Tom. It wasn't long before Young Tom didn't care enough to wonder why they'd taken him or why he couldn't go back to Juneau. Before long, he'd made friends with several of the other boys, and he'd learned how to lie, and how to laugh at the preacher's prissy hands, and how to take a whipping and pray for an hour when he was being punished and Haines House wasn't so bad.

Another war was going on. Tom heard about it at school, and listened to the teachers telling the boys that when they became old enough they would be given guns to fight for their country. He'd heard that more and more people were beginning to say they didn't like the war, and he'd heard that you were supposed to call those people hippies and chickens. The teachers said that if you loved your country you Fought for Freedom and The Flag. Love it or Leave it, they said. Young Tom wasn't sure where he'd go if he stopped loving his country and was told he had to leave it, but he was ready to fight for the United States of America and The Flag. When he turned eighteen, he left school and went to Juneau to enlist in the army. He didn't take the time to walk over to the village or down to South Franklin Street to ask around for Old Tom, even though they hadn't seen each other in almost eight years.

The doctor at the Indian hospital looked at Young Tom from over the plastic rims of his eyeglasses. He put down the little anteater flashlight he'd poked in Young Tom's ears. "I can't sign the paper for you, boy," he sighed.

"The paper?" Young Tom asked. He wasn't sure what the doctor meant, but whenever a white man mentioned a paper it was probably bad news.

The doctor smiled. "I'm afraid it looks like you have a benign neoplasm of the middle ear. Do you experience tinnitus in one or both ears?" He wheeled around Young Tom to look in his other ear.

"Tinnitus?"

"This one looks good. Ringing. Ringing in the ear, do you get that?"

"Sometimes."

"What about your hearing, do you have trouble hearing?"

"I can hear."

"Well, it's a progressive condition, and it's going to prevent active service in the military, son. You won't be able to enlist. The army won't take you."

Young Tom had never thought much about the ringing in his ears. He thought his hearing was just fine. But he trusted that the doctor knew what he was talking about, and he left the clinic without the paper the doctor said he'd need. With no backup plan, Young Tom went looking for his father.

Seated on an empty cable spool down at the boat harbor, Young Tom waited. The place where he sat smelled of tar. Every time he rearranged his legs, the spool tipped with his weight, making a tapping noise that added percussion to the waves lapping against barnacle-covered poles alongside the dock. In the air, seagulls coasted and once in a while called messages he didn't understand. One seagull landed in front of him as he rolled a handful of gravel around in his palm, the gravel's pebbly touch smudging his daylong boredom. The gull watched him out of one sideways yellow eye. Young Tom stared back for a moment, then threw a single pea-sized stone at the waiting bird. The seagull opened its wings and after a couple of ungraceful hops it flew away. Young Tom thought it seemed unsurprised. He wondered if it had wanted something from him.

An extra-low tide had pitched the ramp to an unusual angle. Young Tom recognized The Admiral, older and still mean, walking down the steep walkway from the parking lot. She gripped the handrail as though she meant to strangle it. "Boy!" she called. "What are you doing there? Who are you?"

"I'm Young Tom," he said. "I'm waiting for my father."

Just like Old Tom used to tell him, eating twice a day with only a peanut butter sandwich or a jelly sandwich in between was hard to get used to, but being on the water was good. Sometimes the captain stopped the boat to send a couple of men in the skiff to shoot a seal. On those times, the captain allowed the crew to eat seal meat, along with the bycatch of rockfish, salmon, and sometimes halibut, the always-present pot of rice, and maybe some canned peas. In the morning they drank strong coffee and ate boiled mush. And the smell of the ocean, the feel of the spray, the sound of the gulls, the taste of the salt, the sight of mountain behind mountain behind island behind island, falling back and back in shadows and grey and dark green — Young Tom got used to that right away. It was a good life, being on a boat.

At the end of that first fishing season, Young Tom had a little money. Not as much as he'd hoped; after the crew-share formula The Admiral laid on him and the extra charge for all the food they bought right before the last trip, he had a good deal less than he would have earned on another boat. But he lived in the old house in the village with Old Tom, and they didn't have many bills. Young Tom had enough cash to last the winter with a little left over to go down to the bars on South Franklin and act like he was old enough to drink.

It was at one of the bars that Young Tom met Lucille. At first she seemed friendly but not really interested. She liked attention, liked to dance, liked it when men spent money on her. Tom didn't know how to dance very well and didn't have much money, but he had considerable attention and he gave it all to her. After his second season he had more money but he still couldn't dance. By then the bars he went into were used to him and his money and didn't realize or didn't care that he wasn't yet twenty-one. Being away at Haines House for a few years had paid off after all: people had lost track of his age. Even Old Tom wasn't clear on Young Tom's age. Young Tom worked extra hours at the end of the season, saved more money and sneaked more food off the boat, flashed his money around Lucille and brought her home one cold night. Old Tom was nowhere around. Young Tom built a fire and got some ice cubes from the tray he kept in the cooler outside. He poured orange juice and vodka into two glasses and tried to act suave. Lucille didn't take much persuasion.

"I've been waiting to be alone with you," she said. Her words were slurred and her eyes unfocused. Young Tom wondered if she remembered who he was. "I don't have any panties on," she whispered in his ear. He could smell the vodka on her sour breath; she slobbered a little on his cheek while she whispered. Suddenly she poked her tongue into his ear, causing in him a disagreeable feeling that at the same time excited him. The spit evaporated and he worried about earwax. She grabbed his crotch and moaned, impressing him with her false tone and strong grip. She unzipped his pants and stuck her tongue in his mouth.

That she was clumsy and drunk relieved his anxiety. If he fumbled or came too fast she might never notice. He pressed her down onto the cot. She had panties on after all and her make-believe wiggling made it difficult for him to find a good handle. She continued to moan. He wished she'd shut up and lie still, pass out or something. All at once she did seem to tire; she lay unmoving as though struggling for a second wind, continuing to moan but in a sleepy, halfhearted voice that soon turned into a soft snore. In a few short minutes, Young Tom was in love.

Their baby was due at the end of the season. He was hoping for a boy. If it turned out to be a boy, he'd name it Tom, after him and his father. Tom the Third. Or maybe Tom Three. Something modern. He hadn't wanted to go on this trip, had wanted to stay in town and help Lucille, keep her healthy, try to keep her sober, but she had insisted that he leave. Even when her pregnancy showed, she went downtown whenever she felt like it, taking his money or going without money, drinking and dancing and disappearing with men stupid and drunk enough to think a pregnant drunk woman was exciting. Young Tom hated leaving her in town, but the truth was they needed the money, and Young Tom didn't feel half the man with her as he did when he was out on the water. So he left. That was three months ago. He was on his way home now, the boat stuffed with a last load of salmon in the fish hole. He was anxious for them to sell the fish so he could be off the boat.

The captain would make him wait as long as he could to cash out. It didn't matter to the captain or to The Admiral if there were bills or a new baby. After finishing as much work as the captain could force, Tom left the boat carrying a gunnysack full of fish and seal meat and some canned goods he'd hidden away during the trip. It was enough to tide them over until they let go of Young Tom's share.

He rushed home. Letting himself inside, he smelled a baby at once. Quietly he walked to their bedroom off the kitchen, listening for any sound. As he approached he heard the grumble of a baby at the breast.

The baby squirmed and rooted at Lucille's swollen breast. In the bright room, Young Tom saw clothes and dishes scattered on the floor the way they were in the weeks before Lucille pressed him onto the *St. Patrick*. "Is it a boy?" he whispered, standing perfectly still.

"No," she answered. "A girl. Patricia. I named her Patricia."

Lucille was already going out to the bars again. Young Tom couldn't stop her. It was he who stayed home to watch the baby most weekends. On the nights he could find a babysitter, he walked downtown and searched the bars. More often than not she was nowhere around, most likely drinking under the docks or at somebody's house, but other times she'd be in one of the last two bars that still let her in. He'd watch her drink and hang on men and dance suggestively and walk out of the bar with someone else, staggering by without even seeing him. He'd buy a bottle and sit on the curb or take it home and drink it there. In a year or two, Young Tom no longer felt young.

When little Patricia started kindergarten Young Tom was moved to get sober. By that time, Lucille was just someone who lived in the apartment he rented in the Channel Apartments a block or so from the village. For the next five sober years, he cared for the little girl, met with her teachers, tended her when she was sick, janitored in the winter, and fished during summers, when he left her with her mother, receiving his wife's promises and believing, believing, that the child was safe with Lucille.

The spring when Patricia was ten, Young Tom noticed that the girl was getting tall, was beginning to look like a little willow tree. Lucille became more resentful of the girl, throwing magazines and clothes at her, calling her brat and bitch, grabbing her shoulders and making blue fingerprint-shaped bruises on the girl's arms. Through all this, Patricia seemed to want her mother more. She tried to crawl into her mother's lap, smoothing Lucille's straggling hair, petting her sweating brow. She brought her beer from the refrigerator, cigarettes and matches from the table, paper towels from the counter to wipe up her phlegm and drool. At times Lucille acted affectionate and grateful, but most of the other times she either ignored the girl, or worse, yelled and namecalled and slapped her. One time she even spit on her. Patricia only cried more and begged for her mother's love. Young Tom had been sober for five years.

He went out as usual on the *St. Patrick*, hoping to make good money. Fish prices were way up, openings were hard work, but even the captain had to write a big check for the crew; as big as the checks were it was only a small portion of the whole haul. The captain and The Admiral got rich, rich enough to buy a new house on a fancy road a little ways out the road on a white man's street. They drove a new car, bought a second new car for their oldest daughter, and went to church every Sunday, piously placing five-dollar bills in the plate, making sure everyone saw how holy they were, sharing with the Lord the money they chiseled from the crew.

Young Tom felt rich too. Lucille thought he was rich, demanding money, lying and saying the girl needed clothes or medicine or a toy, stealing it out of his pocket when she couldn't get hold of it any other way. She kept most of his cash when he went out for the summer, telling him she needed it for rent and food while he was gone. He left meekly, not wanting a fight, knowing she'd make a scene or throw things or hit him if he resisted. It was easier just to let her have the money.

He still worried about the girl. That summer they got back to town more than a week earlier than he had told her to expect. Young Tom jumped right off the boat and went straight to his house. It was about ten o'clock on a Thursday night. He thought the girl would be in bed, maybe a babysitter watching her, maybe Lucille at home for a change; her habits were bingelike and she often went several days between bouts of three or four days of being drunk and a day or two of being hungover.

He could hear the raucous activity half a block before he came to the place. He half expected the police to be there; they'd been called for noise to his place so many times it was almost routine. But tonight there was only music and the flickering of a television. He let himself in the un-locked door and looked around the dim front room.

Lucille lay sprawled across the lap of a man Young Tom recognized, a panhandling bum from Ketchikan by the name of Mike. The man was laughing and pouring beer into Lucille's gaped mouth while the warm stuff dribbled down her chin and neck. They jumped when Young Tom turned on the ceiling lights and snapped off the stereo. In the sudden quiet, he could make out the sound of his daughter crying in the next room.

I finally crawled away from the father of two of my sons; he kept my chil-dren, my clothes, our house, our furniture. He put his name on my oldest son's birth certificate, tried to take my name off the house we'd purchased together, and refused me entrance into our home unless he was there. He told the children I'd left because I didn't love them. He broke into my tiny apartment and stole all the clothes I'd purchased to replace all the clothes he had kept. He stalked me. In the middle of the night, he crept up to the little blue Toyota I'd managed to retrieve and poured sugar into the tank. The next morning he showed up to wipe his finger in the sweet granules near the gas cap before I started the car. He tasted his finger and frowned. "Somebody sugared your tank," he said.

When I refused his offer to fix it, he peeled out in his white Buick, spraying mud and dirt on me and my car as I stood in the alley, almost beaten. I swore I'd rather die than live with him. A few nights later I gave in. A doctor had diagnosed my condition as clinical depression and had prescribed an antidepressant. I swallowed all the pills, drank a bottle of iodine, and washed it down with a six-pack of beer.

In the middle of the dark night I awoke. I could move only my right arm, which I raised a few inches until it fell heavily back to my side. The lights to my stereo glowed red in the black night. I thought, I'm still here —nothing has changed, and fell back into a dreamless red iodine sleep.

Early the next morning he came to the door. He looked at the empty pill bottle and the tipped-over iodine and the rest of the beer. He took off his pants and shirt, soothed my sweat-stained hair away from my brow, and leaned forward to whisper in my ear, Take off your clothes. From the deepest part of my belly, I scraped the lining of my resolve and pushed him off the cot and into the alley, throwing his clothes after him and bolting the door. I'd rather die than go back to a life with him, I told myself, and made plans to put my head in the oven as soon as I wasn't so groggy. That afternoon I woke to a knock on the door. Social service workers responding to his call checked me into an observation ward, where I stayed for three days and then drove to Nevada to live with my mother for the rest of the summer.

After a summer-long graveyard shift spotting keno tickets at the Carson City Nugget, I went back to California and demanded custody of my children. We moved to Nevada City, a little gold rush town higher in the mountains, where I met Gary and enjoyed a kind of freedom while my life spun out of control. My mother retired and came to live with me, but she was no more willing to offer advice than she had been throughout the years. She never spoke a word to me about my drinking, my iodine-laced call for help, my children. She kept her own counsel through all our grief. I adopted a mixed-breed dog at the pound and took everyone down to the Yuba River, where we swam and played in the California sun.

Gary and I get a slow start out of Seattle. We stand at the Interstate 5 on-ramp hoping to make it to Olympia with the morning rush-hour traffic, thumbs out and smiles on our faces, until well past the commuter traffic hours. Finally around ten a.m. a man in a blue four-door stops. We pile in and are on our way.

"Where you headed?" the middle-aged driver asks.

"Well, we're going all the way to California, but right now we're hoping to get to Olympia," I pipe up. "How far are you going?"

"I can take you right outside Olympia," the man says. "What are you going to California for?"

From the back seat, Gary sticks his face into our conversation, already tired of being ignored. With a grin, he interjects, "Yeah! California, man! We're gonna pick some flowers!" He laughs and starts humming. "If you're going to San Francisco . . ."

I frown. "We're on our way back home. We live in California, and we've just been visiting in Washington for a while. We ran out of money before we thought we would, so we have to hitchhike back." The driver merges the car into oncoming traffic. Satisfied with his driving, I continue. "Originally I'm from Alaska, but Gary here's from San Francisco. That's why he thinks it's funny to put flowers in your hair. He's just trying to be funny."

The driver's name is Bob. Gary and I have agreed that when a man is driving, I sit in the front and it's Gary in the front for a woman driver. Whoever sits in front makes sure we haven't climbed into the car of a suicidal maniac or a drunken divorcée. Whoever sits in back is supposed to be ready to spring to the defense of the other if necessary, not sticking his face between us making a limp joke that no one thinks is funny. "We're going to go over to Highway 1 and stay on that as far as the Bay Area," I tell Bob. "Then we'll take Highway 80 up to the foothills. That's where we live. We want to see the Coast Highway, though. It sure is beautiful." Friendly small talk is a rule of the road.

Bob glances at Gary and smiles. "No problem. I was in San Francisco for a while. I know what it's like." We settle into an observant silence. I try not to look at Gary.

Before long we're piling out of the sedan and saying our thank yous to Bob. "Thanks, Bob!" Gary hollers and waves while I look around for a good place to hitch our next ride.

Choosing a place to stand and thumb for your ride is key. Optimally, the location must have a long approach so oncoming drivers can notice you and check you over well in advance. There should also be a proximate straight stretch where a driver can slow down and stop safely after deciding to give you a ride.

Making the best use of that approach time is the sign of a seasoned hitchhiker. Stand straight. Remain attentive. Appear friendly and harmless. Smile, but don't look goofy. Make sure your appearance is tidy. Tuck all your gear at your feet in a small pile within easy reach. If a car slows down but doesn't stop, make eye contact and do your best to look normal and calm, even though you've been standing on this godforsaken strip of paved hell ever since Bob let you out of his car a good four hours ago. When a car slows down and you've made eye contact but it passes anyway, keep watching it. A driver might stop after he's passed you, and you must be prepared to grab your gear and run with a big grateful smile as fast as you can to the car, keeping up with Gary, who is running faster on longer legs in front of you, and who would leave you behind if that was his only reasonable choice, no matter how sincerely he denies that he would ever do that, no matter how ardently he professes his adulterous love.

When a car has slowed down and stops half a football field past you and then peels out just as you get there, redneck teens laughing and calling insults out the windows as you come to a resigned stop, bags dragging, gasping for air, legs cramping, disappointed—migod it's beginning to rain—you must resist the impulse to curse and wave them the bird, giving as good as you get. Take only a moment to gather your strength, look at one another, shrug your shoulders, and pick up your heavy bags. Calmly return to your strategically chosen point. Tuck your gear around your feet. Compose your face into friendliness. Stick out your thumb. Even though the rain is now streaming down your weary face, look as normal as any drowning cat could do. Be glad those hippie-hating teens didn't come back. Be glad they didn't give you a ride.

We climb gratefully into the next car that stops. It isn't long before we realize that hitchhiking down the two-lane coastal highway is going to be made up of hours of waiting interspersed with a string of short rides with occasional coast dwellers running to the store for gum. More often than not we wave at them going back the way they came an hour later, grim smiles still on our faces, bags still tucked neatly at our wet feet, getting desperate, getting hungry, and, against all my efforts, getting goofy.

"We'd do anything for a ride!" I call, smiling lips unmoving, as cars speed by. "Stand on your head again!" I holler at Gary. "Do something funny so they'll want you inside their car!"

Gary kneels on his backpack and situates the top of his head on the gravel at the side of the road. "Ouch!" he complains. His legs wiggle as he raises his knees and he falls. A bicycler wheels by. Gary jumps up. We stick out our thumbs. The bicycler, who had already passed us twice before only to be overtaken twice by our own short leapfrog rides, ignores us. He only thought we were funny the first time.

"We'd do anything for a ride!" I call to his vanishing back, and turn to Gary. "I have to go to the bathroom!" I scold. "I have to pee. I'm hungry, I'm tired. I want to go now."

"Go over there in the bushes," Gary suggests. "That's what I did."

"No you didn't," I argue. "You went right alongside the road, I could still see you. You're lucky a car didn't go by." I feel like picking a fight. Only days before, we made a wary truce to try to stay together. To forgive and forget. But I know I can never forgive him for his week of unfaithfulness when he went to Victoria without me. The thought of his betrayal rises in me like bile unbidden throughout every day. Like bile, it gushes into my mouth from the bitterness inside me. Like bile, I spit it out. "You don't care—you'll pull that damn thing out anywhere!" My voice rises. "You can't even keep it in your pants alongside the road!" I shove his shoulder, cruising for a fight. "You slut," I namecall. "You're nothing but a slut."

"Oh, Babe," Gary coos, hangdog. He's in the wrong. His only way out is to throw himself at my mercy. Affectionate charm is the only thing that will work on me now that honesty, faithfulness, and a realistic hope for the future are shot all to hell. "Oh, Baby," he babykiss whispers on my cheek. "Just go over there in those bushes. I'll watch for cars. Nobody will see you." He pats my shoulder.

"Oh all right. I can't wait any longer. Call if a car comes." I highstep through the coastal shrub over to a goodsized boulder and pee in the already wet sand. "Is a car coming?" I call.

We travel down the Coast Highway through Washington and into Oregon. We sleep in our sleeping bags inconspicuously near the road that first drizzly night, still in Washington. We rise early the next day, catch a quick ride into some small coastal village, wash up at a gas station, splurge on a country breakfast, drink too much coffee, and head out again at midmorning. By the end of the second day, we're only about halfway through Oregon. At this rate it'll take days to make it to the Bay Area. Our progress is slow, the fun wore off halfway through the first ride, we're running out of money. When we drag ourselves out of a truck on the other side of Newport, our experience and fatigue tell us to find a place to camp. We'll get some sleep and rethink our plan in the morning. We're too tired to want to eat anything but whatever we're already carrying. It's stopped raining, but we're damp and chilled in the sea breeze.

We straggle along the road and soon we see a likely place to camp. A small sandy ledge just below the road halfway down to the water looks protected and dry. We can hardly see it from our standpoint; it looks difficult to reach, anyone trying to get to it would make enough noise to wake us. We climb down and set up a little camp as dusk falls, constructing a soft base for our bed from green shoots of iceplant and dark dried seaweed. We break out the last of our grub: a box of raisins, beef jerky, a small block of cheddar cheese only a little bit softened by the heat of Gary's body as he carried it in his pocket, ready for us to take a nibble now and then throughout the day. We are both thirsty. There is only one orange juice left from the two containers we'd been willing to carry.

We snuggle into the sleeping bag at sunset. We share our strong-tasting jerky, nibbling slowly for the pleasure of chewing as well as for the flavor. We sip our juice, passing the carton back and forth, our fingers deliberately touching each time we trade it. Below us the lights of the harbor blink on one by one. Blue and red navigation lights jewel their way toward the open ocean. Running lights of small boats entering the harbor flash around the piers. Lights inside live-aboards shine homey and friendly. All is silent. The clearing sky unveils a fingernail moon above the pale horizon. Moonset. The gentle tidal water in the harbor reflects the lights of the boats and the buildings and the buoys. All is quiet.

It had been touch and go for a few days, but little Patricia was finally over her fever. The doctor at the Native clinic released her from the hospital with pills and warnings and a frown. "Just take good care of her," the stethoscoped white doctor had cautioned. "Patty will be fine with rest and plenty of fluids." Now Patricia watched Tuesday morning cartoons with lively interest; she looked at her schoolbooks, and she wrote notes to pass to her friends from fourth grade. Her appetite was back.

"Daddy, can I please have some more fried potatoes?" she asked. She wiped her brown hair away from her face. Her hair hung straight, greasy, more stringy than before.

"You ate it all up," Lucille said. Tom collected the bowl and spoon from the table near the couch where his daughter lay and put clean sheets on her bed, throwing the sweaty spotted sheets onto the pile of dirty sick clothes. Lucille sighed like a martyr and said he'd better carry the whole load to the launderette tomorrow. "Have some bread and butter if you're still hungry," she told the girl.

Patricia liked to roll the bread into a ball and eat it like a donut hole. "Can I have some sugar on it?"

"There's no sugar, either," Lucille said, not looking in the cupboard. "You ate all that up, too. Maybe I can borrow some from Charlie next door. I'll go see." She picked up her cigarettes and walked out, letting the torn screen door slam behind her.

Young Tom got the bowls and plates soaking and gathered the fevered sheets and sweat-wrinkled clothes into a bundle and tossed them into the cold hallway. "I'll get you something sweet when I go down to the boat, little girl," he promised his daughter. "I'll get you a piece of candy at the store."

Young Tom stayed at home as much as he could. But he could walk down to the harbor and on the way back he could stop at the store for some jellybeans. He needed to check with the skipper anyway. It wouldn't be too long before they'd start working on the nets, getting ready for the next opening. It was always a good thing to stop by at the boat, see what was going on at the harbor.

Buzzy the first mate, his brother Skip the cook, and Harvey the deckhand, were making themselves comfortable on the deck of the *St. Patrick*, trading stories of last year's catch and next summer's fishing. When Young Tom joined them, they were laughing about some of the white men they knew, a favorite subject, not caring that White Man Jerry was on the next boat, tending to his gillnetting gear, listening and laughing and chiming in with jokes of his own. Jerry was just like a Native man anyway. He preferred Native women in his bed. He lived in a little house in the village. He drank, he was almost always broke, and he laughed at everything. How much more Native can you be, everybody thought, except maybe the Native women part. Plenty of Native men, Young Tom included, liked white women. But not when their wives were around.

Young Tom had some white friends, mostly from fishing boats. He noticed that whenever he said the words "white people," a lot of his white friends acted like he'd said something unfriendly. What do they want me to call them, he wondered. There weren't names for white people the way there were for Indians and blacks and people from China and Japan. White people didn't see themselves as anything but people. They should be called pink people.

"Hey, you're not a white man, you're a pink man," he called over to Jerry. Jerry laughed. He laughed at himself a lot. That was one more thing that made him Native.

"White people are crazy, anyway," Skip said. Skip was an old crew hand who had worked with Old Tom years ago. "They have everything but they don't even know it. They like to think they don't have anything a Native man couldn't get."

"How about white skin, can I get that?" Buzzy said. Over the winter, most of the guys got jobs around town. But Buzzy's dark skin and thick black hair blocked him from any but the lowest jobs. Low man on the totem pole, he laughed when he couldn't get hired.

"White people have everything, but they don't like to hear it," Skip said again.

Jerry called from the next boat. "I'm a white man. I don't have everything." He popped open a can of Rainier and passed around a six-pack, just to soften things. Young Tom let the six-pack go by. Everyone noticed. A couple of the guys nodded in recognition of Young Tom's choice. More for them.

"My grandma used to call it privilege," Harvey said. Harvey lived with his mom and his dad in a nice house up the hill in a fancy part of town.

"What do you mean, 'privilege'?" Buzz said.

"She used to say it was a privilege to move into a white neighborhood or go to a white people's church."

"That was a long time ago, though."

"My grandmother's still alive. She's out at the Pioneers' Home, they let her in even though she's not a pioneer." Harvey took a sip, burped, and was silent for a minute. "There's still white neighborhoods," he said. "White churches. White jobs."

"Okay, it's a privilege to live in your neighborhood. I always thought so anyway."

"I'm still white and I still don't have everything," Jerry laughed. "I don't even have another beer! Pass it around, you guys."

Young Tom picked up the remaining beer and passed it back to the next boat. "I know one thing white people have," he said.

"What's that?"

"They have their pictures all over the money."

"What about nickels?" Buzzy said. "Isn't there an Indian on a nickel?"

"Yeah. A nickel's worth of Indian for every dollar's worth of white man."

"Black people down south call it power," Harvey said. He watched a lot of news on his parents' television.

"Right. But up here it's white power, not black power."

"It's privilege, just like Harvey's grandma said."

"Well, what else is there?"

"You guys kill me," Jerry said from the next boat. "I only have one more six-pack."

"Pass it around, Jerry! You know you don't count!" Everyone laughed and helped themselves to Jerry's beer.

Twenty years down the line, Gary would have fit a description for a Detroit rock-and-roll wild man: straight blonde hair hanging past his shoulders, skinny bald chest, blue-eyed devil smile, Fender air guitar always ready to wail. But that kind of rock and roll was still a twinkle in the Motor

City's eyes, and Gary listened to Santana, Bonnie Raitt, and J. J. Cale, from whose songs he took his self-image. "They call me the breeze" filled Gary's thoughts and resonated through his weekend plans. He dropped his housepainter's brushes into a tray, waved so long to his boss and sometime best friend Smitty, and took off for the Bay Area to watch the Niners play a home game at Candlestick, his constant best friend Smokey showing off a big lab/setter smile in the back of Gary's pride and joy '71 Chevy long-bed. Before heading out, Gary stopped at the store for a six-pack of Pauly Girl and a can of mixed nuts, and I went along for the ride, helping him study this week's stats and lobbying for Creedence instead of the breeze.

Al gimps unevenly across the unpainted floor over to the chipped wood desk, his brown polyester pants only a little bit crumpled. He rests his Bo Peep cane against an open drawer and pulls out a camera. I watch him push his dark-rimmed eyeglasses closer to his indifferent eyes, adjust the camera's focus finder, and pull out the white lip of the shine-treated film. "Stand up," he says, not bothering to look at me.

I'm perched on the edge of a worn faded cushion, holding my Sunday-best shirt and my 36-C black bra in my lap. My feet hurt. It's been a long time since I've squeezed them into t-strap fuck me shoes. I admire my newly painted bright red toes. I've always been vain about my shapely toes, except for the one that is so much shorter than its neighbor. Polished and peeking out from under the thin bare straps of unwalkable shoes, though, they hold their own against my reckless tits.

There's already a run in the pantyhose I splurged a couple of bucks on at the Woolworth's store at the corner of Market and Powell where cable cars clang themselves in circles and turn around to head back up the hill, tourists and locals hanging off the sides and sitting on smoothly polished benches inside and out, gawking in jawdrop interest at the sidewalk parade, at all sorts of folks walking up and down the hill, Market to Geary, Geary to Post, Post to Sutter. A man with curled overgrown fingernails clicking his unchallenged path, varnished women in tailored wool coats clenching shopping bags from Union Square boutiques, men kneeling at the corners, cups and signs begging while they point their chins into the air and maintain a sort of borderline dignity, telling themselves they don't see the civilians walking by tossing them coins for their conscience. Desperate women in paisley shirts and fuck me shoes.

I drop my shirt and bra on the green cushion and look at Al. "Lift up your skirt," he tells me. I lift my skirt. I have to get this job. If he doesn't give me a job, I'm not going to let him keep a picture of me standing here like this, pantyhose and rhinestones, all my plans as desperate as uncovered breasts and puppy-eager toes.

"We keep a photo in every file," he says. I blink at the flash. "You start tonight for the midnight shift. Show up at 11:30." He pulls out the photo and snaps the camera shut. He sticks the picture into a file without waiting for it to dry.

I've worked a graveyard shift once before, when I spent the summer as a Keno dealer at the Carson City Nugget. I don't look forward to it. I'll have to find somewhere to sleep; the homeless shelter where I crash has an eight o'clock curfew and during the day changes itself into a raucous food line. But a job dancing topless in a place where the sign reads Girls! Girls! is the best I can do until I get some kind of bankroll. At least I won't have to worry about what to wear.

For the first time in my life I've lied about my age, peeling off five years and telling an uncaring Al that I am only thirty-two. But it's not my accumulated years that betray me. It's the sagging and scars from inconstant life and three children. But Al has seen the faces of women beaten and strung out and days from death. He doesn't see me or my years and scars and sags.

I work three weeks at the Girls! Girls! place, long enough to get a paycheck that enables me to rent an efficiency apartment on Turk Street, use the public phone as a message number, apply for a typing job, and get hired at an insurance company in the Financial District at One Hundred California Street. I go from a place where the sex is so thick you can cut it with a spoon to a place where the people look like they don't have zippers in the front of their pants.

During the three months I work at the insurance company, I feel no different from the way I felt every time I danced on the revolving floor to the rhythm of frayed curtains winding up and down as men behind them fed stolen quarters into the slot, or every time I talked on the telephone to a window-framed customer in a private booth, listening to him say the things he longed to say to his wife or his neighbor or his mother. Whether it was sweating at the dance parlor or typing at the insurance company or posing for Al while he indifferently adjusted the focus on my life, my thought was always the same: nobody sees me. I am the only one in this room.

Lucille was gone for a few days before Young Tom started to wonder where she was. Usually he'd catch word of her being at some days-long house party, or at the wino camp under the docks if the weather was good, or in jail. But she left one morning, saying she was going next door to ask their neighbor Charlie for some sugar, and Young Tom didn't see her again. After a few days he went next door to ask Charlie what he knew and found out that Charlie hadn't seen her in a week. After that, Young Tom asked around and put it together that Lucille had lit out on a fishing boat on its way north. She'd left word for Young Tom that she was going back to her family. She left no word for Patricia.

Young Tom would rather get drunk than tell his baby girl that her mother had left her without even saying goodbye. The first time Patricia asked for her mother, Young Tom walked back down to Jerry's boat and asked him for a drink.

Jerry looked at him for a minute. "You sure you want to do this?" he asked.

"I need a drink."

Jerry lifted the cushioned seat lid and pulled out a six-pack of Rainier and a pint of cheap vodka. "You okay?" he asked Young Tom.

"I need a drink."

The smooth finish of the boat's lightweight table already suffered from the stains of bottles and cans and soup bowls and knives covered with butter and lint. Jerry set the beer and the vodka between them on the table. They sat facing one another and looked out the curtained window at the empty *St. Patrick* tied up at the next stall. Jerry pushed the six-pack toward Young Tom and waited for him to feel like talking.

The man who'd introduced himself as George is businesslike. He wraps his lean, tall body into an industrial uniform, fits a plastic helmet over his crewcut, adjusts the poison-tank on his back into a comfortable position, and goes to work. He points a long nozzle at the shelf above our heads, waves us back a few feet, and begins to spray. At once, poisoned cockroaches rain down in sheets, falling onto the plastic face of his helmet. Gary and I stare in fascinated disgust. George slowly moves the nozzle along the shelf while hundreds of cockroaches fall on him, bounce off, and land on the living room floor not even twitching. My jaw has dropped open so I cover my mouth with my hand. Even though the spray has no odor, I'm sure it must be potent to be able to kill those resilient survivors we've been fighting for such a long time — it must be almost a week now.

We've moved in as new managers of a building on the corner of Ellis and Taylor in San Francisco's Tenderloin District. For keeping the public areas picked up and the garbage taken out, we're to receive a two-bedroom apartment rent free. When we heard about it we thought it sounded like such a good deal that we took it sight unseen, even though Gary and I are familiar with the Tenderloin and should have known better. Especially me. Unlike Gary, I've slept in Tenderloin flophouses and stood in food lines more than a few times, and I know that all our feeble battles against rotten piling garbage are already lost.

Kitty-corner from the building is Glide Memorial Church, where Reverend Cecil Williams wows the congregation every Sunday morning he's in town. After a rousing service, everyone separates into two main groups: those that file out the front door to shake hands with the Reverend, mostly dolled up older ladies impeccably dressed, balancing shiny hairdos, with pint-sized patent handbags hanging calmly from one bent chocolate arm, and the rest of us: wrinkled, hungry, and down on our luck, filing in the other direction, lining up for the free Sunday meal that Glide serves, thought by many food line connoisseurs to be the best in town. Living right across the intersection, we know we'll be in a position to have dinner any day we choose. That plus a free apartment sounds like Easy Street. But it's just the Tenderloin.

At first I'm startled every time I see a cockroach run across the wall when I turn on the light or when I see a cockroach fall out of a sleeve when I unhook a favorite shirt. Gary, on the other hand, makes it playtime — he constructs little cockroach motel villages and recruits them for little cockroach football playoffs in excited anticipation of college and pro-season games soon to come. In only a day or two, though, my surprise turns to dread and Gary's playfulness is replaced by a bitterness I've never seen in him before. But I can't hold it against him, since he's the one who has to shovel the broken garbage tossed noisily down the chute into the basement dumpster every night.

"You should see the ones in the basement," he always responds when I marvel at the size of a cockroach I've found in a shoe or a sleeve. "That's nothing. The ones downstairs will only run away if I pound on the floor with a shovel, and even then you can hear them running." His blue eyes take on a crazy look, and it isn't the happy kind of crazy that has won from his friends the affectionate nickname Crazy Gary, it's the haunted crazy look of a man who has witnessed the unspeakable. "They're as big as little mice down there. Their feet click when they run. You can hear them!"

"That's really bad. What should we do?" I pat him softly on his sweet bony knee.

"Let's just get out of here," he suggests. "Let's just split."

Splitting is something Gary's good at. It's always his first choice. I'm afraid one day he'll leave me for good in just the same way. "Maybe if we called an exterminator," I counter. "We don't have anywhere to go, where would we go? Let's try to get the owners to call an exterminator." I call the owners, who call back to tell us to expect an exterminator the next day.

George finishes with our apartment and the hallways and apartments on our floor, then works his way down the building's four flights all the way to the basement. He promises that the cockroaches will stay gone for at least a week, possibly two weeks. In a week or two he'll be back to spray again, he says, and then we'll be cockroach-free for two or three months.

"When they do come back," he warns, "they'll start in the basement and on the lower floors. They won't get up here to the top floor right away at all." This is more reassuring to me than it is to Gary.

As I'm sweeping up piles of dead cockroaches, one of the tenants taps on the door. "Yoohoo, Mr. Gary-Gary!" calls a falsetto voice. "Yoohoo!" We can tell it's Cookie, the most forward of all the transvestites who live here in the building.

"You get it," Gary whispers. He avoids Cookie's girlish attentions. When Gary was given fresh cookies last night and invited upstairs for a drink he panicked. "What a weird guy," he had said. "Why would a guy want to dress up in a nightie?" Something tells him not to make friends. He declines Cookie's offers and invitations with an aw-shucks self-conscious embarrassment. "You get it," he stage whispers again. "I don't want to talk to those guys."

"I can't. I've got to clean this up and then sweep the hallway and then go down to Mr. Yosef's apartment to get it ready for him to come back. You do it."

"No, I don't want to. I don't like him."

"Quit being a baby. She probably just wants to give you more cookies," I laugh. I open the door and excuse myself around our visitor, who waits in the hall in peignoir and gown, holding a plate of cookies. Cookie looks at me as though I'm one of the cockroaches and bats fake lashes at Gary.

"Here, Mr. Gary, so much thanks for getting rid of those terrible roaches. Mr. George he was wonderful, he loved my cookies, but I saved these ones for you." Cookie holds out the plate to Gary as I walk down the hallway dragging my scruffy worn broom to sweep the halls and stairs.

Later on we line up at Glide for dinner. I've swept and mopped all the floors while Gary read football magazines, and we did laundry and took showers. We feel encouraged, clean, hopeful. "We have to give the garbage men the new key tonight," I remind Gary. We've been told that the garbage men come around 2 A.M. and that they need keys to the new lock right away.

"Well I don't think I want to do it," he says. "I have to shovel it all every night, that's plenty. God, I hate garbage. I hate this whole place."

"I'll leave them a note," I say. "One of us ought to be able to stay awake till two."

Gary falls asleep after watching a preseason game, snuggling into clean sheets. I turn off the television set and try to stay awake. The garbage men won't be able to take the garbage unless they have a new key. Gary will mutiny for sure if they don't take it. I have to stay awake.

It's a weeknight so the traffic calms down around midnight. Outside the living-room window, large neon letters flash the name of the girlie club below. On the sidewalks, dark lonely shadows appear and disappear slowly, in halfbeat time to the neon's flash. Down the street, figures in front of an overpriced grocery and liquor store laugh and poke one another, sizing up the men and women who enter the store. Everything becomes more and more quiet. Everything moves more and more slowly while the red neon letters continue to flash.

The garbage truck appears at the corner from outside my view. I have just enough time to grab the keys and quietly race down the stairs out the taped-over broken glass door and down to the corner. Several yards from the corner stands one of the garbage men hunched over the note I've left, straining to read it in the dark, trying to make out my words. I approach him, holding out the new keys. He takes them from my hand without a word. He turns away to unlock the door to the basement dumpsters. I walk back to the apartment. I watch them make their way up the street toward the grocery store, where the small crowd watches them slowly go by. I creep into our clean bed beside Gary, happy to spoon him and sleep.

Mr. Yosef's apartment is built around the large interior shaft between buildings and has no view and no sunlight. But even so, there is a strange glow throughout the whole front room. A tattered couch and a few end tables are arranged around an old television set. The one window is poorly covered by a ragged curtain and half-drawn torn shade. The small lamp on one of the end tables is tipped on its side, the browned old shade bent and rusted. Miscellaneous tin cans and brown bags and crumpled newspapers and what looks like old food are scattered all over. Covering every surface is a layer of several inches of some sort of fine sawdust that appears to be giving off the golden glow. I examine a pinch of it, rubbing it between my fingers. It's smooth, almost like lanolin. I wipe it on my shirt and go inside.

Leaving the door open, I track through the slippery substance and peek into the kitchen. The tiny table, the refrigerator, and the chair are all covered with the same stuff. An old calendar on the wall shows a smiling blonde woman in a fifties-style hairbob. The date reads August 1959. Right month, but off by almost twenty-five years.

Mr. Yosef was taken to the hospital a few days before and can't move back in without some serious cleaning here. Two days ago the community health program called to let me know that Mr. Yosef would be able to return to his apartment soon.

"We're having the place exterminated tomorrow, so maybe he should wait until after the poison is gone," I'd suggested. "I'll take a look at his place after it's exterminated, and make sure it's okay."

"That will be fine," the voice said. "We'll call when we're sure what day he'll be released."

When I go back to our apartment for a broom, the phone is ringing. I pick it up, looking around for Gary. It's the community health lady again. "Good news! Mr. Yosef is ready to come home tomorrow," she says.

"I don't think he should do that. His place doesn't look ready, it's all dirty and messy, I don't know if I can get it clean that soon," I say. "I just came down here for a broom, I'm going to try to sweep it, but he can't come back yet. I don't think it's even really healthy at this point. It's pretty bad."

"Is there somewhere else for him to go?"

"I don't know, I don't even know him, I'm just the cleaner, basically. I've only been here a few days."

"Well, his condition doesn't warrant his remaining in care, his psoriasis is quite severe, but we're satisfied that if he continues to apply the topical salve we've provided, the scaling and inflammation will decrease and he'll be comfortable."

"His what?"

"His psoriasis. He's got quite a severe case, but he's responding very well to treatment. In a few weeks, his symptoms should begin to diminish. His prognosis is quite good."

"Psoriasis? You mean like, skin?"

"Yes. He'll be able to come home tomorrow."

"He can't come home tomorrow. You need to find somewhere else for him to go. You really should send someone to look at the place before he comes back. I mean, I'll see what I can do, but I know I won't be able to get it clean by tomorrow. Sorry." I hang up.

I let myself back into Mr. Yosef's apartment and look around at the slick golden layer, the accumulation of years of scaly skin. There is no way in the world I'll be able to sweep it all up with my pitiful broom.

I stand in the center of garbage and scaled-off skin and watch a cockroach crawl across the face of the woman in the calendar. She keeps smiling as though she doesn't notice the filthy thing polishing her once-white teeth. Looking straight at me, she lets me know by mental telepathy from her 1950s blonde and blue-eyed calendar brain the unmistakable message, illustrated by the return after only one day of another stinking cockroach on the wall, that things just aren't going to get better. I drop the broom and run to find Gary.

He isn't in the apartment. His football magazines are gone. His favorite shirts are missing. I run to the window, look up and down the street. In front of a parking lot on the next street on the way to Market, I see him leaning against his pickup, leafing through a magazine, for all the world a happy man. I run down the stairs and down the street. "Hi, Babe," he says.

"What are you doing?"

"Nothing."

"Where's all your stuff?"

"In the truck."

"Are you going somewhere? Are you leaving? Weren't you even going to tell me?"

Silence.

"I can't believe you're just going to leave me in that rotten place to take care of everything myself! What about the garbage? How am I supposed to take care of it?"

Silence.

I point a finger at him. "Don't go anywhere!" I run back to the apartment and grab my things as fast as I can. Like Gary with his magazines and shirts, there are only a few things I really need. It takes me less than five minutes to collect my handful of belongings. I waste half the time running to the window every few seconds to make sure Gary is still waiting.

Gary gets in the driver's seat and starts the engine when he sees me coming. I pitch my things in the back of the truck and jump into the front seat. I wait until we're well into traffic before I start ragging him. "I can't believe you were going to just leave me there by myself! How could you do that?"

"Want a beer?" He gestures at a bag on the seat between us. "I bought some Pauly Girl."

"Where are you going?"

"I don't know. Let's go up to the mountains, get some fresh air, see Smitty, see how Smokey and Gypsy are doing. Let's go hiking or something. I've had enough of this place for a while." He raises his eyebrows and smiles at me sideways.

Getting back up to the mountains sounds good. I open us each a Pauly Girl while Gary puts on some music. We wheel over the Oakland Bay Bridge to the sounds of Santana. We hit I-80 to the tune of Boz Scaggs. By the time we get to the foothills, we're singing along with Creedence Clearwater's "Born on the Bayou," glad to be alive. Glad to be together. Glad to be gone.

Patricia's fifth-grade teacher asked a friend of hers, a woman named Mabel who worked as a grocery clerk, to go to Young Tom's apartment down on South Franklin Street and check up on the girl. Mabel knew Patricia and Young Tom and Lucille, and she was a caring woman, so she went. When she found the girl alone, she persuaded her to let her in, and she cleaned up the apartment and they went shopping, and back at the apartment she cooked a meal of hamburger and fried potatoes for the girl. After dinner, they washed the dishes together and decided what to do.

"Would you like to come stay at my place until your mom or your dad come back? I have a television," she tempted the girl.

Patricia examined a thumbnail. She didn't answer right away.

Mabel had plenty of Native friends and neighbors. The silence while Patricia thought about her words didn't bother her. She waited for the girl to make out how she felt.

Patricia bit a nail. She nibbled it with her front teeth. She tasted her words. "All right," she said.

It was only a few weeks before Young Tom sobered up. By then, Mabel wasn't willing to give up knowing Patricia, and although Patricia was happy to see her father sober she was also pretty happy in Mabel's comfortable place in the Fosby Apartments, not far from the governor's mansion overlooking the village. Young Tom started coming by every day, and one morning he was still there when Patricia set off for school. Later that year, she saw papers for a divorce. Young Tom explained to her that Lucille had sent a letter saying she wouldn't be coming back for a while. Patricia wrote a letter to Lucille asking if she could call her or come see her, but the short answer she got a few weeks later told her nothing except don't call and don't come. Patricia stayed with Mabel, and Young Tom stayed sober and got a job as a bagger at the same store where Mabel worked. They spent more and more time with each other, and by the time Patricia went into junior high school, Young Tom moved in with them and the next thing she knew they were married.

Young Tom was happy. He was doing pretty good at being sober again, and with Mabel at his side he could do anything. She didn't care what people said when she fell in love with a Native man and he stayed in her bed overnight and they got married. She took good care of Patricia even though the girl got sassy and wild and by the time she was thirteen was staying out later and later until one night she didn't come home at all. Whenever Mabel tried to talk to Patricia, the girl only yelled and name-called her, hollering that Mabel wasn't her mother like it was the worst kind of accusation.

He didn't know what to do about any of it except try to stay sober. He got to where he was relieved when Patricia didn't come home even though he heard from his shamefaced friends that there was nothing she wouldn't offer to do for a drink. By the time she was fourteen she was pregnant. She brought the baby home, recuperated for a few weeks, and one night she was gone again. When she came back months later she brought another baby and left again. Grandpa Young Tom, a boy and a girl. Mabel loved those babies more than the world. She'd never had her own children, and Patricia was a sorry disappointment to Mabel's dreams of maternal love. But those babies were hers, no doubt about it. And Patricia was happy to leave them with Mabel.

Young Tom fell off the wagon when the second grandkid was born. He stayed drunk for a couple of years, living in the village in abandoned cars with Old Tom, watching Patricia stagger by with different men, her hand in their pockets, her mouth at their ears. Mabel let him come home when he felt like it but she wouldn't let him drink there. He lost his job as a bagger and went out a couple of summers on the *St. Patrick*.

One of the new hands, a young man named Norman, was a pretty funny fellow who liked to make fun of people. "Old moocher," he called Old Tom. "Young moocher!" he called Young Tom, and rocked the boat with his own laughter. He made fun of everyone in such a good-natured tone that no one took offense. "I'm sure getting tired of these white people," he pretended to worry. "They act like they own everything." He'd hold a straight face as long as he could, then belly laugh. "Hey Tom," he'd holler. "What's the difference between herpes and true love?" He cracked himself up over and over with the same old jokes. Everyone liked Norman, but he was new in town, and he didn't really know his way around.

One night Norman saw Patricia standing around outside the bar and made a joke about her. That was when Young Tom decided to sober up. Patricia was eighteen that year, and Young Tom never wanted to need a drink so bad that he'd laugh at a joke about how many beers a blow job from his daughter was worth.

I am on my way to a part-time job helping an old married couple in the rural home they've lived in for more than a generation. I've recently broken up again with my best-ever man-friend Gary; my children are with their father or with my mother or on their own. I'm driving the station wagon that soon will carry me to Seattle, and beside me is Gypsy, the black mongrel dog who is my only steadfast companion. It's usually my chore to help the old woman with a bath, chop apples into a salad, pick up the house, wash the dishes. Vacuum the floor. She can't breathe without the oxygen tubes connected to a tank she drags from room to room on her slow slow restless walk. He moves a bit faster than she does, but he can't talk without pressing a finger to his throat and croaking through a device implanted there after he had part of his esophagus removed.

She enjoys telling me her regrets as I help her into the shallow warm bathwater and sponge her white wrinkled back and shoulders. She regrets smoking cigarettes when she was young. She regrets being old. She regrets her marriage. She regrets her life. Seeing these two people places new meaning on the vow Gary and I once made. This is what it would have meant had we kept our moon-eyed promises to grow old together.

Twice a week I drive through the countryside into the Sierra Nevada foothill boondocks to finish my domestic chores as fast as I can, collect my twenty-dollar paycheck and reassure myself that I'm appreciated. But I'm becoming more and more dissatisfied with the routine, and it won't be long before I force myself to give them notice, expecting disappointment. But it will turn out that she's been trying to think of a way to tell me that a favorite neighbor has become available and they prefer her for the job. All will be well.

In the autumn in that part of California it finally rains. Hillsides and mountainsides and gardens and fields soak up the welcome rain. Dust settles. Green things peek out beneath straw-colored roadside firestarter. Leaves of yellow and red and brown float down from the happy trees. It finally rains.

When sprinkles hit my windshield I stop at a pullout so I can stand in the rain. Gypsy runs to the bushes, wagging her butt and bouncing her nose on the ground. Long-missed rain cools my summer-parched face. Gypsy gives me a quick big smile and rushes down to the nearby creek before I can say Let's go. She scrambles away, looking for squirrels or something to roll in. I follow her down to the creek.

Oak and willow line the little creek. It's actually a shallow river, a little wider than the two-lane country road. I stand on a matted cushion of yellow and brown leaves that have fallen from the trees above me. Oaks give off an understated masculine smell, as though the rain has released a special fragrance. Magpies and blue jays scold us for a while, but even they can't stay angry for long. More-distant robins and meadowlarks tentatively resume their rainy-day songs.

The river isn't deep, but the midstream current moves fast. Placid curves along both edges have carved out quiet pools. On the opposite shore where pools rest under the oaks, drops of water splash onto the flat surface and cause small ripples. Rain collects on the branches of the trees on the opposite shore and falls in drops onto the quieted water, making ripples that meet one another and blend into the shore or the current. Drops from the trees and raindrops from the sky make different kinds of splashes. A rhythm is established. Oaks continue their fragrance. Birds continue their songs. Yellow and brown and green leaves splash with the raindrops. Each time a raindrop falls, a leaf jumps. Leaves float down from the trees. Ripples move on the water. Leaves tremble and jump at my feet. Everything sings.

I never spoke anymore about going back home, but it was in my mind every day. I didn't know how to enforce the child support order I'd obtained at the court. All my money had run out, the job I'd found was too many miles away to make any sense. My mother lived in a rented house in Grass Valley, a little town in the Sierra Nevada foothills in northern California. I traveled back and forth to San Francisco, breaking up and reuniting with Gary.

I had finally prepared in my mind the only place I could go. I had pictured myself back home and now I would go there. Gary had decided to move to Lake Tahoe. My oldest son lived with my mother, and the other two were with their father in Eureka. I had only my dog, a rattletrap gold-colored station wagon, and the determined resolve to pay any price to get back home.

Four days after I said goodbye to everyone I loved, I woke during the night. My stomach hurt, an outspoken pain, and I remembered this: an awakening, the thought Well, here it is, I can't sleep, I wondered when it would begin, the perception of pain. Waking to a dark room, the briefest moment of awareness before sinking back into an intensely sound sleep; waking in the early morning to find I'm still here—nothing has changed. And this time, feeling strong, strong enough, secure enough to hold my ground, to regroup my forces, to persevere. It brought to mind that other night: darker, more drugged; a different awareness, a different thought, a deeper sleep; the same thought upon awakening: I'm still here. Nothing has changed. And the seductive evil: do it again do it again. But on this morning I woke to a sure resolve. I was finally homeless; I was finally broke. I was finally forty. I would go home now, or I would die with my thoughts facing north.

The White Lady keeps a prim appearance and fools bored store clerks and rushing pedestrians who don't look closely at her scuffed leather handbag and frayed nylon hose. At the homeless shelter in the early evenings, she spreads a lace hanky on the table and sets her snack like a fancy tea party, holding fast to the thinnest of lines between herself and the blaring insanity. Today we are on the Metro bus, coming back from another unsuccessful day labor call.

"It's just not fair," she announces across the aisle. "Other people have made complaints. I arrive on time and they still don't let me work." A frown interrupts her brow. Her hand tightens. She glances ahead, checking for dangers and threats in the path of the bus. Her mouth grims itself at the edges. "Even when you go in, they might not use you. Then you don't make any money, and you lose your place!"

The young woman sitting next to the White Lady pays no attention. Beth's round, unlined face sparkles untroubled, innocent eyes. "Leave me alone!" Beth whispers to my backpack propped at her side. She disregards the bubblestorm of complaints building in the next seat where we sit at the back of the bus.

"I have other engagements," the White Lady continues. "I should be allowed to use the facilities. My son will hear about this." Her fingers drum the fingerstained post. She glances forward again with greater scrutiny. She watches for suspected but unseen dangers. Her voice changes; she adds a pinch of shrillness. Beth's whispers become louder, more constant. Outside, traffic and pedestrian noises provide a backdrop to the whispers, murmurs, and complaints across the aisle.

Our stop comes up and we file off the bus. Granny, a big dark-skinned woman who sports a mustard-colored umbrella and a permanent scowl, sits in the doorway of Saint Anthony's. Her wide ruffled skirt curtains the crate that keeps her possessions and cradles her big butt. The ruffle along the bottom of her skirt is grey and tattered. Stiff-looking: it's been wet and dried from rain and snot too many times. In contrast, her shirt and her black wool winter coat look almost new. Her once bright-yellow umbrella, reminiscent of southern ladies protecting their freckles from the sun, blooms above her head. She tucks her belongings closer to her fat, bent knees when she sees us approaching. She scowls how-do. I nod in response.

She is alone in line but has cautious company nearby. Snappy-dressed Razor stands a few feet away, guarding the shine on his shoes. He checks his manicured nails and the forming line. He's hoping to notice a naïve girl or needy woman who might show up for easy pickings. "Hey, Baby," he drawls. He looks at my shoes, raises his eyes and his eyebrows to my face, smiles his own how-do. "How you doin', Baby," he greets.

"Not bad, Razor," I respond. "How 'bout you?"

I sense Beth behind me talking to my backpack again. I set my pack carefully in the corner near Granny, my back toward the corner wall. I squat, get comfortable. I'm second in line, Beth is third. Beth's face is blank. Our eyes meet. I epiphanize the concept of nonplussed. She turns away, whispering to her hand.

The White Lady likes to walk up and down the street while the rest of us stand in line. She times it so she places herself at the front of the door minutes before it opens. No one challenges her premise that our immediate circumstances have been created for her convenience and now function at her pleasure. She is amicable if disdainful, and embodies a role no more curious than Granny or Beth. In the evenings after showers, she spreads her lace-edged hanky before her on the table, places a silver knife and fork setting from her large leather purse. Because of its fitness for other purposes, she can never hold on to a spoon. A spoon is too noticeable, and this is a place where being noticeable is danger.

Anonymity is the goal of every survivor here on the street, anonymity for ourselves and for our possessions. For many of us, that anonymity is captured with insanity. We're not easily noticed if we cause others to notice our symptoms instead: our clothing, our behavior, our fears.

The White Lady's insanity is most manifest in her prim presumption that she is normal. She might be the craziest of us all. "My son is a doctor," she announces every evening at snacks. We munch on soggy croissants left over from some lunch place in the Financial District and watch the White Lady perform her high tea. She engages us in socially requisite small talk. "He's actually an ear, nose and foot doctor in Marin County, just north of here." She nibbles her croissant and touches the corner of her mouth with a wrinkled paper napkin. She trembles with the tremendous effort of pretending nothing is wrong. I think about gripping her wrist and making her look into my eyes and telling her: Something's wrong! It would be so easy to sink into the street. First to smile at my secret thoughts—I do that often now. A few words spoken to myself: sentences, stories, fullborn muttered imprecations, a gale of laughter, scowls. Humming to the music in my head. I do that often now.

Our worlds share patches of common ground. Some are killing fields: nobody's land, barren, threatening, uninviting. Some are open zoos, forcing us to be very, very alert. Some are quiet: dark, secret places, the only places where we can touch one another, feel one another's skin. Warmth, soft flesh. Touching is never done in our worlds except in these secret places, on the unsteady common ground of the rocks beneath our bare, cut feet, washed by salt water rushing past with no other purpose than to cleanse.

Those cast here homeless must be orderly. We stand in orderly lines in designated places or we go without food, safety, shelter. We cannot afford to offend the rules. Unexpectedly finding yourself thrown onto the darkening street because of a breached rule is disaster. Always disaster. Only someone truly insane jeopardizes comfort for poor reason.

Saint Anthony's Shelter for Women, operated by the Catholic church around the corner, is a safe and comfortable downtown crash right in the middle of the Tenderloin District. A woman can get a guaranteed bed if she gets in line by six, which makes day jobs and panhandling easier for those so inclined. It's within walking distance of North Beach, Chinatown, the Financial District, Mission District, and Fisherman's Wharf. It's a couple of blocks from the Greyhound bus station; the Civic Center library is only three blocks away. Two fast-food places on Market Street tolerate well-mannered homeless people who have cash. Although Saint Tony's serves two meals to both men and women during the day, in the evenings and nights it's only for women. It's been my regular place almost every night this summer.

We settle in for the next wait. Get comfortable, fit our butts on the floor, on chairs, against the wall. We assemble our belongings, unpack a few things, read, chat, mumble. The first forty women are assured a bed. Everyone waiting on the inside ramp can count on a place to stay if everything else goes okay. If nothing goes wrong. If no one picks a fight and involves innocent others. If the shelter isn't commandeered to house inmates from nearby overcrowded holding cells. Or commandeered to house their victims. If a fire doesn't break out. If the water pipes don't burst. If a bomb threat isn't broadcast and in the melee of evacuation all our places in line are lost. If all the waiting, the patience, the tolerating, doesn't come to nothing after all—as our efforts so often do—then we can count on a place to stay for one night.

I take my yellow pouch of Top tobacco from my shirt pocket and roll myself a cigarette. Carefully sprinkling the stringy unruly threads along paper-thin tissue bent to the shape of my index finger, I diddle with it as long as I can, just for something to do. My companions all watch me, just for something to do.

I'm sitting at a small table, my pack at my feet where I can feel it with my shin, my cash in my front pants pocket, my tobacco in my shirt pocket, my back to the wall, my eye on the door. A young man sidles up, tries to bum a smoke. "Hey, Baby," he smirks. "Got a smoke for me, Baby?"

"No. I haven't got anything to give away."

"Ah c'mon." He invites himself to sit down with me. "I know you got tobacco, let me roll one. Roll one for me!"

His greasy hair is slicked back away from his pimply face, his button-up shirt is dirty at the edge of the collar, a cheap gold chain hangs over his chest. At the end of the chain is a pewter charm of a bighorn sheep. He must want me to think he's an Aries. A Ram. He's a third-class punk, one of the small-time hustlers on the make for someone to latch onto and leech off. Probably a vampire, the descriptive word for the bums who loiter outside the blood bank waiting for a mark to walk out with eight dollars from their biweekly sale of plasma. "Not today," I say.

"Let's go buy a forty-ouncer," he proposes. "I've got about a dollar. How much you got?"

"Nothing. Leave me alone."

"Ah c'mon, you got money. Let's go party."

I look him in the eye. "Not today," I tell him again.

"Hey, no problem. I'm just trying to give you a hard time!" he smiles, turning on the charm. His lips are cracked and peeling, little pieces of dead skin have accumulated in the corners of his mouth.

"Listen," I tell him. "I'm sitting in a shelter waiting for a food line, smoking roll-your-owns. I'm broke and I'm homeless. I'm already having a hard time." I lean forward, look straight at him. "Why do I need another hard time from you?" I pick up my pack, pat my pockets and go outside for some fresh air.

San Francisco's Tenderloin is all about nudie shows, food lines and shabby hotels. A few square blocks in size, it's bordered on the east by the Civic Center, where cement walls allow the forlorn and depressed to while away the time amid the gathered trash blown and kicked into the concrete corners. Whiling away time is the main activity of the people who live here. Every food line has particular hours; loitering outside the doors of the shelters is discouraged. The two or three fast-food places on nearby Market Street enforce a strict time limit on the street people who have saved enough coins to spend on a cup of coffee: two refills with a timed receipt, forty-five minutes to spend inside a warm bustling place and feel like part of the lively scene.

It's not often money well spent: when it's not raining, sitting outside watching life unfold is a far better pastime. During allowable hours, we sit inside the shelter, warming up, drying off, killing time until the next line forms. The Civic Center, with lots of suits passing by and its familiar piles of fast-food trash, offers outside comfort and security. Most people who frequent Saint Anthony's food line hang out here at the Civic Center. They pass around green bottles of Thunderbird, or bum each other's smokes, or they sleep. Sometimes people get sick, they puke, one time someone died. Everybody watches the passing show.

Dorothy and her teenage daughter are almost always here. They say they've been sleeping here, climbing onto the high sculptured blocks near the fountain after dark, dragging behind them a couple of old sleeping bags and several shopping bags filled with their belongings. When I ask why they're not still sleeping at Saint Anthony's, they tell me it's because Amy, the daughter, hasn't signed up for school yet. The shelter won't let children stay unless they are registered to attend school.

"That sounds reasonable," I say. "Maybe she should go ahead and go to school." Amy is chewing the ends of her hair and scratching her scalp. She's dressed in wrinkled cotton pants and a brown T-shirt that sports the slogan "Celebrate Ghirardelli's" above a picture of a big, smiling chocolate drop.

To while away the time, I've twisted and ribboned my hair into two thin braids to frame my face. When Amy sees that I have some ribbon left over, she asks me to braid her hair. Her mother is a skinny unkempt woman with a dingy complexion who blames all her ills on an absent husband recently fled. I'm tired of listening to Dorothy's complaints, but she's taken a shine to me and makes a point of sitting and standing next to me at the Civic Center, in the food line, at the shelter. Dorothy lights a tailor-made and kicks aside the trash.

"Amy's going to get into school pretty soon," Dorothy says. "I'll sign her up as soon as the welfare is okayed."

I twine ribbon into Amy's hair. It's fine and chestnut brown; her freckled face nods when she hears her mom talk about school. "Yeah," she says, "I'll be a sophomore if I get in before the end of October. Otherwise I'll have to be a freshman again." It's the middle of September. She still has time.

Odd translucent dots speckle the strands of Amy's hair. "This is funny dandruff you have," I tell her. "Have you washed your hair since you've been sleeping outside?"

At Saint Anthony's we are required to shower and wash our hair every night. We have to check in by seven, shower by eight, and wait for bedtime. Local sandwich places often send over their unsold goods; we're regaled with croissants almost every night. We're not allowed to make our beds until eleven, and lights out isn't until midnight. We wake to the blast of a blaring radio and the smell of brewing coffee at six. We're always tired.

"We haven't had a shower since Saint Anthony's kicked us out," Amy says.

"Well, you better do something about this dandruff, it looks really funny." I examine one of the dots on my fingernail.

Joe, a kid of twenty or so, walks up and sits by Dorothy. His thigh rubs against Dorothy's leg. She blushes. Her hormones drift off her like a plum tree shedding pollen. She simpers and bats her eyes at the boy. His shirt is unbuttoned almost down to his waist, showing off a sunken, hairless chest. He's wearing new blue jeans and a pimpy red hat. He takes a cigarette from Dorothy, inhales, leans back.

"That's not dandruff," Joe says. "She's got lice."

I rip my hands away. "Lice! Oh, great, I touched her hair. I touched my hair. Is that why they kicked you out of Saint Anthony's? You have lice? I can't believe you let me touch your hair!" I wipe my hands on my jeans, grab my pack, take off down the street.

"Where you going?" Joe hollers.

"To the clinic to get medicine. I can't afford to get head lice." I walk fast across the Civic Center, past the courthouse, double-time to the other side of the municipal buildings. In a little alley I find the free clinic and sign my name on the waiting list. Joe and Dorothy and Amy follow me in and write their names on the register.

Amy sits beside me, still my friend. "Thanks for braiding my hair," she says. "I really like it." She smoothes her braids, bats her eyes at Joe.

"Are we sleeping at the fountain tonight?" Joe asks Dorothy, smirking.

"We have to," Dorothy frowns. "They won't let us back into Saint Tony's for two more weeks."

"I can't believe you didn't tell me. I braided her hair," I scold.

They look at me blankly. Dorothy goes outside for a smoke. Joe moves over to Amy, rubs his leg on hers, glances out the window, whispers something in her ear.

An attendant calls my name. I follow her into the examination room and tell her my story. The doctor doesn't want to give me medicine until I actually have symptoms but I talk him into it. I get the medicine and walk out.

I go to one of the sleazy hotels in the Tenderloin and spend most of my last few dollars on a cold room with a thin dirty mattress and one bare bulb. I wash all my clothes and my pack in the dim basement laundry room. I hack my hair into an uneven crew cut. I take three hot showers and when the hot water runs out I take one last cold shower. In the morning, scrubbed and liceless, I think about showing up at Saint Anthony's for breakfast, but I decide to treat myself to breakfast at Glide's.

Glide Memorial Church is more strictly run than Saint Anthony's. Saint Tony's is Catholic. Glide is Southern Baptist. Glide features the Reverend Cecil Williams, guitar music, shouting. Their helpings aren't as big, but the food is clean and fresh. Glide Memorial is all windows, stained glass, bright-yellow walls. We march down the line, served by all-business black men wearing transparent plastic gloves. I two-step to the nearest open table to eat and leave, taking my plasticware with me. Behind me, the table where I sat is already wiped and smelling of bleach, ready for the next hungry person treating herself to breakfast at Glide's.

More food is served in bigger helpings at Saint Anthony's, and their serving hours are longer. I hurry straight from Glide to Tony's so I can have a second breakfast there. I walk down the wooden ramp into the windowless basement. At the bottom of the ramp, I'm handed a token by a bored volunteer and enter the havoc. Hands wave, dishes clatter, people shout, servers scurry. I find a seat at one of the long tables and hold the yellow plastic coin above my head. This is the same hall where we eat croissants at night, where mattresses are spread for sleep, where I hang out in the evening, listen to women argue, watch TV, gossip, wait for a shower, wait for a bed. The workers and volunteers spend more time here putting down tables, picking up mattresses, moving chairs, getting out supplies, picking the tables back up, putting the mattresses back down, folding up the chairs, putting away the supplies, than is actually devoted to providing shelter to the women who call this, if not home, then at least home base.

I continue to hold up my plastic coin. Eventually one of the servers tires of ignoring me, having served all his friends twice, and brings me a tray bearing a plate piled with cold reconstituted eggs, scrambled dry and colored green. Next to the eggs are the Saint Tony's staple, mashed beans. It's not one of my favorite meals, but the toast isn't bad and the coffee is hot.

After breakfast I walk up the ramp and lean against the entrance wall to roll a smoke from my pouch of Top tobacco. I watch people go in and out of Saint Anthony's. I talk to a few people who make jokes about my mangled hair. I laugh. Later on I'll walk down to the Civic Center and watch the suits walk by. Maybe I'll head over to the library. I'll while away another day.

Now Chamai—she was a deadhead. She reeked of the Grateful Dead the way her long skirts reeked of Humboldt skunk. Colorful silk scarves loose around her waist, long straight hair braided with beads and twined with feathers, barefoot, she strutted and twirled down the street announcing to one and all that she was a medicine woman, a mystic. She told the world *Here I am!*

She lived in a cabin on the Ridge and traveled back and forth to town in an indecisive old Jeep painted camouflage, its hood missing, tires bald, exposed engine coughing and sputtering and shaking the car and everyone inside. She'd been born in the Aleutian Islands at the end of the Second World War, given an American name, and raised by American standards. She'd had two baby girls while she was still a girl. But she wasn't allowed to keep them, those babies. Those baby girls. She was persuaded by family and church to give them up. Then she took off for California. Haight-Ashbury in the sixties. Flowers. Love. She took a new name, which means "hello" in the old language. It was the only word she confidently recalled.

In San Francisco she had a baby boy, his father a black musician. She named that baby Antelope. A couple of years later in the Sierra Nevada foothills she had another baby boy by another musician, this time Hispanic. She named that baby Yuba. She raised those boys on organic gardening and the Grateful Dead.

By the time we met, her boys were almost grown. Together we went to shows in San Francisco, hitchhiking to the City and staying in the Haight with old friends. We saw Greg Allman, John Cipollini and George Thorogood in the clubs and danced at Dead concerts in the park, then we hitchhiked back to the foothills, taking come-as-you-are rides, laughing, telling stories, reliving the music. Everywhere we traveled, I saw her tell the world *Here I am!*

Over the years she had wondered about those baby girls she'd given up so long ago. When she found out they'd been adopted in the states, she joined a locator service and saw no reason ever to go back to an outdated world where she felt she'd never belonged.

Late one afternoon that camo Jeep pulled up on the street in front of the shelter where I slept when I was homeless in the City. The motor jumped and sputtered while her two boys kept it running. She climbed out of the Jeep and ran to my side. "Guess what! I found my girl. We're going to meet her right now!" We hugged and smiled, her feathers dancing. Then she jumped back into the Jeep and they bounced away in a cloud of patchouli, her braids waving a happy goodbye.

I saw Chamai again a few weeks later. That daughter had been adopted into a self-righteous, intolerant farming family in the Sacramento Valley. Whatever that girl's fantasies about finally meeting her birth mother, they must have been instantly crushed when she saw a long-haired hippie woman pull up in a camo Jeep, Creole and mestizo half brothers alongside. The visit had been strained, kept secret, quickly finished. And Chamai's beloved daughter had told her never to call again.

"I found my other daughter last week. We're going to see her in Santa Cruz." She glanced at her waiting sons. "What if she doesn't like us?" Chamai couldn't buy a new car. She couldn't dress differently. She couldn't leave her sons at home. All she could do was show up and say *Here I am*.

A few days later I watched that camo Jeep sputter up the street one final time, the boys and Chamai inside with big smiles all over their rainbow family faces. Chamai leaned happily out the window as they drove slowly by. "Guess what!" she hollered. "My daughter loves us! I have grandchildren! Black and Hispanic! We're all going to a Dead concert this summer! Love you! See you! Goodbye!"

I never saw Chamai again; I guess I never will. Her willingness to meet her second daughter after the grand disappointment of the first was true courage. Her success with that second daughter was true good fortune.

I wandered in the darkness and I heard a woman cry. I saw that woman get her baby back. Knowing her became a gift. I saw the substance of courage and good fortune, and I learned that sometimes it's enough just to show up in this world. Just to show up in the world and say *Here I am.*

Young Tom stayed sober for a couple of years. He'd sobered up and was living back at home with Mabel and the babies one day when he walked to the grocery store and who did he bump into but Nadine walking toward town with his friend Norman. "Where's Auntie Susie?" he asked her after they hugged and admired each other.

Nadine stepped back and admired him again. "My mom's living on her own up in the Mountain View Apartments," she told him. "You should go see her, I'll tell her you're in town." She put her hand on Norman's arm. "We should go, we're going down to the Arctic, do you want to come see us later?" The Arctic was one of the Indian bars.

"Maybe later," Young Tom said. "I've been sober for a couple of years, though."

"Well, that's good," Nadine said. "I saw your dad, too bad he's still drinking." She gave Young Tom one last good smile. "I should quit, too," she said. Nadine and Norman walked away, headed to town.

A few months later, when the town was rich from all the workers who went north to Valdez to get paid big money to clean up all the oil all over everything from one of those tankers that spilled millions of gallons and destroyed in a few hours what everyone thought would take at least a few more years to ruin, Young Tom just gave in when Harvey offered him a drink. Young Tom had gone up to Prince William Sound when they put in a call for Native workers but the smell of the oil had made him too sick. Or maybe it was the sight of the beach and the rocks covered with thick black poison. Or maybe it was all the dead birds. Or all the seals dying. Or the bruise he got on his thigh when he slipped on the poisonous muck. Or all the white men telling him what to do.

Why were they still in charge? he asked himself. They elbowed their way in to shit all over everything and then they elbowed their way in to tell everybody how to clean up all the shit. Young Tom threw down his cleaning rag and went back to Juneau. The next time someone offered him a drink he took it.

With the grandchildren old enough to be in school, Mabel wasn't as easy with his drinking anymore. She didn't want the children to see him or Patricia when they were drunk. With Patricia that wasn't much of a problem because she acted like she didn't have kids anyway. But Young Tom tried to leave town whenever he felt a bender coming on.

He caught rides over to Hoonah, a Native village a few hours from Juneau, and stayed there and drank and sometimes he camped and fished or hunted. He borrowed a skiff and caught fish and explored and thought about his days on the *St. Patrick*. He thought about those days with Lucille and about those long-ago mornings with Nadine and Susie and his mother. This time, he planned to drag the skiff onto the shore, drink the beer he'd brought, cover himself with a tarp, wake up in the morning, finish off the vodka, catch some fish, and go back to Juneau. Clean up for a while. Take some fish to Mabel. Get sober. Try again.

Young Tom dragged the skiff onto the beach, unloaded his tarp and his gear, and glanced at the sky. Low clouds promised rain. Slippery rocks formed a bed where he tied the skiff at high water; at low tide it would be nestled in the stones, loosely anchored, waves barely reaching the stern, their gentle lapping keeping time to his drunken crooning, the skiff rocking in a pleasant invitational dance as Young Tom polished off the beer he held, even when drunk remembering to save most of the vodka for the morning to knock the edge off his fuzzy never-sober hangover and yesterday's resolve to make a better life.

The Bog

At sunrise before the Raven calls, a woman enters the forest. She is fat with child. Inside her belly are all of tomorrow's generations.

Although now is the time for spring, patches of snow and ice still create danger. The woman must be careful where she places her steps. She vanishes into the forest. How will she survive? How will the child survive?

In a house in a far village, a young woman wakes, remembering sounds in the night. On a trail at the distant side of the forest, a young man walks, not sure of his way. In nearby waters, men and women run to the shore and vanish into the still-dark forest. Perhaps they will meet the woman. Perhaps they will simply be lost.

Occasionally someone disappears into the woods. Now and then a body is recovered, sometimes without a head. Having disappeared into the forest, a person might never come back. The wild call from inside them may have captured them.

There is a man who lives in the forest. Signs of him can be seen in chips of wood around a tree, usually a sapling. This man carries a hatchet. Grandmother says she never heard anyone say that he will hurt you, but stay away from him anyway. Avoid all wild men in the forest, especially if they carry hatchets. But nothing is said about the men who carry as their weapons meager hearts and troubled natures.

We might have survived the wild man in the forest; we might have run or charmed him slowly from his blade. But the ones who brush our shoulders on the streets, who touch our hands, who caress our brows and cut out our hearts, have left us headless.

My mother's earlier life had made her swear she'd never go back to Alaska, and my sons were California boys, but I stuffed my pack with a change of clothes and a couple of books and I hitchhiked to the coast, where I retrieved my old Chevy wagon and my dog. The years had disappeared. My home had fallen apart; my children were gone. My possessions had all been lost or abandoned. The only thing I seemed to have left was that happy little mutt I had rescued from the dog pound years before. I planned to live in San Francisco in the Tenderloin, working at day jobs, standing in food lines and sleeping in shelters, until I had a bankroll big enough to get me to the next town. In this manner I was determined to make it all the way up the coast and home, living in my car for most of the way.

In September, I pulled into Eureka after driving all night, my dog snoozing at my side. It looked like a good place to spend the winter. I found a food line that served every day. My dog was most often the first to be given a plate, piled high with our first glimpse of that day's meal. She made more friends than I did. She had more fun. Every day, she waited patiently outside the door while I cleaned my plate. Her new friends brought her scraps; kitchen workers filled her plate. After every meal, she and I sat in a nearby field covered with wildflowers and dewdrops and waited for evening.

In October we joined a fishing crew and went long-lining for three weeks on an albacore boat. I saved enough money to make it to Seattle. But I wanted a chance to spend time with my youngest son, who lived nearby with his father. It was difficult to work around all the restrictions and rules: I was not allowed to go to his home, and I had to depend on my son to make his way downtown for an occasional visit. I had only the smallest hope of seeing him, but I decided to wait in Eureka until after the holidays.

When I woke up in my car that Christmas Day, the foghorn was the only sound that I could hear. No traffic. No music. No voices. The unwelcome damp kept me in the car until it was time to show up for the midday meal. I walked to the hall with my dog and tied her up at the door. I went inside and lingered over my Christmas turkey-on-a-tray.

I recognized some people standing in line for second helpings—not usually served. It made me happy to think we would have a special Christmas treat—a second serving. But when I went again to the front of the line, the server recognized me by the wrap I always wore. "No seconds until everyone else has firsts," she said.

I turned away empty-handed. Others in the hall unwrapped small presents and called holiday plans to one another. Their happy smiles sparkled under the bright lights. Laughter mixed with holiday tunes coming from the kitchen's radio. "Merry Christmas," someone called to me.

"Thank you," I said. "Merry Christmas to you."

I retrieved my happy dog and we walked to a gazebo in the middle of downtown. We sat on a cold cement bench under the octagonal ceiling. The fog crept close. The streets were empty. Everyone but me had someplace to go that Christmas Day.

My dog sat at my feet. She watched my face for signs of play. She wiggled her eyebrows, she rolled her eyes. She licked my hand, she nuzzled my knee. She shivered.

I had never seen fog so deliberate. I had never seen streets so empty. I drew my wrap around me and gave my dog a kiss on her warm and caring face. I scratched her cheek. I missed my family. A warm place to go. The smell of cooking. Lights, a ready bathroom, a door to close behind me. My mother. My sons. After a while, we walked to the car to wait for evening. On New Year's Day, we left for Seattle. Eventually we made it all the way back home.

There were only two food lines in Eureka. The food line I frequented most often was a kitchen that served at midday. Later on in the darkening evening we walked to the car and we slept. The other food line served after dark, so I almost never ate more than once a day. The only overnight shelter in Eureka was a church-run private home with a limit of five days; every morning, every afternoon, and every evening was filled with prayer and sermons, enough to drive me back to my station wagon in only three days and back to the food line, where my dog was welcome and I was permitted my own convictions.

In Seattle were any number of food lines, but no shelter that seemed safer than my friendly gold-colored station wagon parked at the end of the downtown trolley line. The old car was finally at the end of her miles, having chugged and smoked and been pushed the last few yards to a parking space that had no meter, where my dog and I slept every night undisturbed until May.

We settled on a food line in an alley not far from an Indian bar named the Hawaii West. It wasn't the best food by far; the accommodations were no more than shaky tables crowded among boxes in a cavernous storage room, but most of the patrons were Native and it made me feel closer to home. The workers loved my dog and always served her before the rest of us were even allowed inside. We waited in line in the alley, straining for our first glimpse of the day's menu generously piled on Gypsy's plate in front of the alley door, where she was loosely tied to a wooden pallet, making friends right and left, wagging her happy tail at the sight of that day's macaroni and sauce.

I sometimes walked uphill to a Sunday food line open only to women and families. I enjoyed seeing all the children, and the food was home-cooked and delicious. Almost every time I went, there were plenty of leftovers and I was given a foil-wrapped package to carry back to my car. But I didn't go to that food line very often. My chronic ulcer acted up the whole time I was in Seattle, and I was often exhausted by the uphill walk.

I boarded an Alaska state ferry in Seattle early in May and arrived in Ketchikan on Mother's Day. I called my mother in California with the glad news: I'm in Alaska. She took the news in the same style she'd always received news from her only daughter — nothing could surprise her, nothing could impress. Nothing would dismay. Nothing would delight.

The Salvation Army provided the only food line in Ketchikan, serving on weekdays only. On weekends I lingered at the Seaman's Center, where snacks were sometimes offered and fresh-picked berries sometimes shared. On the way back to camp, a companion and I fished off the docks of one of the harbors, catching white-fleshed rockfish that we grilled at a make-shift campstove in the trees on untended property just south of town. My youngest son, now a teenager, had flown up from Eureka to spend the summer in Alaska. We ate fresh fish with handout day-old bread and foraged greens, leaning back after our meal to count the eagles above the waters of Tongass Narrows. We stood in the Salvation Army food line and fished off the pier and picked huckleberries. It was the last food line I'd be in for a long time, perhaps for the rest of my life.

At summer's end, the quickening dark snapped me back to my senses and I got a job, an apartment, and my own kitchen, where I cooked my own meals and planned my own menus, hardly calling to mind my days of standing in food lines up and down the West Coast. But if I ever had to, I could stand again in some food line. I would anxiously wait for a glimpse of the day's meal, looking forward to the possibility of an extra serving. At the end of the meal I'd walk back to my car and keep myself warm with my memories.

Behind the southeast wind a woman's voice is wailing. I lie alone in the night hoping to hear. Steadfast, charming sorrows soothe me softly into slumber, until a distant sound startles and I am wide awake listening. Did I hear, a moment ago, a woman crying? But the sound becomes the whistling of the wind, or an animal's moan, or silence. In the middle of the darkness, in the middle of the night, I comfortably renew another regret.

I paint in my mind a cabin in a forest: a garden, a woodstove, a creek. I sip homegathered teas while I join the seasons' evolutions: peacefully shadowed winter mornings, recklessly long summer evenings, the ocean, a garden, the mountains. I paint us companions, as needles from the cedar are companions to the forest.

The music of the Taku Wind spirals down the mountains to skip on the ice-cold channel like a flatsided stone of air, then smoothly respirals up the next mountain to the other end of the Gordian knot, all the while shrieking and moaning, a compelling windsong all the while in its wake. I hear a song older than this life's distant childhood. Inside that sound are other notes, notes that are always new. The cry of eagles is one of these sounds; the noise of gulls is another. A familiar chorus from faraway childhood, one that is always new.

I see other things in the water: the time to dig for clams or look for fish, the time to stay on land for fear of drowning, the time to engage the day. The water reflects the sky; each spirit in the water becomes part of the day. Between them, fog marries water and air, brighter than both. The mountains draw my eyes from every perspective. My eyes find rest there.

There is the water, there are the mountains, there is the land. From the land I gather berries, celery, teas. Also from the land come deer meat and bearskins. Where water and land unite appear clams, seaweed, crab. From the air float the feathers of birds; earth and air embrace and there appear eggs. One becomes oneness. In a blended moment I find mortal comfort in the rotting of the forest. All around me it rains.

Raindrops fall on pine needles, the pine needles jump. Every time a pine needle jumps, a moment goes by. Every moment is older than this life's regrets; in every moment is the marriage of earth and her path.

The mountains on the nearest islands shield me from open water. They protect me from the surer fate of becoming a Kóoshdaa Káa. They remind me where it's best for me to stay. I often look to the distant mountains to perceive the mountains I call mine. The snowline is as high as it ever rises, the rest of the mountain is trees. The forest is thick all the way to the beach.

Inside the forest it is never bright. Rays of sunlight are defined here and there among the ferns. Jacob berries modestly reveal themselves on the forest floor, devil's club and bushes of every kind push me toward the nearest creek. Here I find sunlight, berries, fresh water, a path. I can follow the path of the creek into the forest or down to the beach. I can stay where I am, sunning myself in a patch of red huckleberries, listening for eagles and perhaps other things. I lie on a soft grass carpet in the sun and suck the juice of berries. I take off all my clothes. Water makes music on the rocks, birds worry and brag out loud.

Fall soon changes to winter. The long month approaches. Days are short; dark months whisper soft calls, pushing clouds and wind before them, warning all who have not yet returned to winter camp: now it is time to go home.

Sunset came a long time after the glaciers first decided they would go all the way back to the mountains where the night is long. Even though the sun was beginning to set, the place where the glaciers had been was still in bloom.

Imagine a land once covered with glaciers, now covered with bloom. Imagine the breeze at the end of the day, soothing the dancing blossoms, teasing them because it loves them. Imagine their colors, blue and purple tinged with white and green, slowly fading with the evening light. Slowly fading with the autumn cold. Quickly releasing all their seeds onto the waiting earth, who receives and embraces and nurtures this next genera- tion. The seeds will wait.

Not much allows itself to be seen in the cold white snowcovered day- light. Not much movement. Not much life. The glacier is still. It bides its own time and it keeps its own secrets. The ocean moves as it always has. On the other side of the water, mountains fall behind mountains and island falls behind island.

The winter daylight is bright, but all the colors beneath the clouded sky are shadowed in gray and dark green. The sky on this day is cockle- shell gray; the beach is overcast brown. The winter's ocean waves are mys- tery blue. The lowest edges of clouds are summer-dirt white; they match the tops of the mountains, which urge themselves to reach and touch and become a part of the sky. Here or there the suggestion of yellow or red re- veals a dried secret blossom or berry. In every other place, under the snow it is green.

Green is the color of the froth that floats on the waves and deposits itself on the intertide to dry and crack and frame the print of the trail of the gull or a raven searching for food. Moss growing on the beachside rock peeks out of the fracture where it broke the basalt a Raven's day ago, flushing the cheeks of the petroglyph's face to a bashful green. An eagle lands on a cedar snag; the highest branches submit. The eagle looks down on the canopy and for a moment sees nothing but green.

The fragrant cedar are not the only old growth trees in this forest. Spruce and hemlock and moss-covered pine thicken and rot. The hemlock branches will be especially good for enticing egg-fat herring to deposit their roe. After the herring have finished, the branches will be white. Rinsed or not, the eggs will be good to eat raw or steamed. Either way, a few stray hemlock needles will inevitably be caught in a mouthful of eggs.

When Raven went in search of daylight, he turned himself into a needle from a tree and caused himself to be swallowed by a trusting young woman. That needle must have come from a hemlock branch: the hemlock needle is used to being swallowed. It is another good taste of green.

In the field near the beach, clover will bloom. In the clearing not far from the muskeg, Hudson Bay tea. These and other plants will sustain a good life. In the dim shadows, skunk cabbage will hide. The bear and other creatures will find it delicious. They will prepare their greens in this way: they will bite off and chew.

Where water and land unite will appear pungent clams and seaweed. From the air will float the feathers of pacified birds. The sky will fill with eagles; ravens will come quite close. Their calls and cries and gossip will fill the air. On every side it will rain.

Inside the forest it will never be bright. Rays of sunlight will define uncovered ferns. Jacob berries will modestly reveal themselves on the forest floor; devil's club and bushes of every kind will push toward the nearest creek. Here and there will be sunlight, berries, fresh water, a path. Underneath the snow, all will be green.

Essential balance manifests in the Raven side and the Eagle side. This balance is seen in the ceremonial reciprocation of ear-piercing, burial, marriage—in all the roles inhabited by opposites. Clans establish our relationships. One says "There is my grandfather" when referring to others of her grandparent's clan, no matter their age. It is with the clan that the relationship endures.

Ceremonies affirm our relationships with one another, with the salmon, with the land. Ceremonies may differ in significance and display; big ceremonies, called invitations, are held for central events, especially those in memorial to a very important person now dead. But smaller ceremonies are also held, parties for persons whose wealth cannot support a big invitation, but whose memory is no less precious.

Balance inhabits reciprocity. Everything will be answered. Nothing attains substance until it is received by the opposite clan. When the box of tradition is opened, the Eagle and the Raven fly out of it together.

The land around the mother village was carved long ago by glaciers, as was most of Lingít Aaní. We know this because there are stories that tell of some of the people coming down the rivers in the direction of the ocean. On one river, the people came over the ice. On the other important river, to the south, the people came under the ice. It is thought that when they got to the shoreline, there were people already here. It is thought that instead of warring, it was decided by those wise ones that they would form one people, in two sides, and to cement their new social order, it would be their practice only to marry someone from the other side. In only one generation, they were one people.

At a place outside Klukwan, three strong rivers converge. They travel down the melting mountain-glacier against the glacial tide, in a cycle the length of which is rivaled only by the history of the people whose generations travel with it. As the glaciers pulled back in their never-ending forward/backward dance, they left small pebbles scraped into a large alluvial fan that receives the rivers' flow to the irresistible sea. All along this large flat fan, pebbles lie in shallow rest. Waiting. The rush of the rivers has become comfortable with the gathering of the gravel. The rivers gather here as well.

In the winter, when the small streams and even the larger rivers are joined by the white snow, temperatures drop and the waterfalls on the sides of every mountain slow and then freeze in midfall, becoming tall slick frozen moments of rushing stillness. The salmon are spent. The freezing water will not welcome them, and will not shelter their eggs.

Except here, in this good place. This place where three rivers meet, where pebbles have been scraped across the fan, this place that has a recent memory of the glaciers sliding over its face. In this place, the pebbles at the bottom of the rivers have trapped fresh water within the pockets formed by their rest against one another. As the water above them tries to freeze, these little pebbles release the water they hold, and it bubbles toward the surface.

The gathering of these forces keeps the water warm and open. The salmon who come from this stream are able to return even after winter has laid itself on the surface. Under the water, it is still warm enough to shelter the eggs of the next generation. And although the bears have gone to their winter place, the gulls, the people, and the eagles gather here at this alluvial fan near the mother village, to take advantage of this late run of salmon, this last, this last gathering of the salmon.

Eagles gather here. They feast and share the bounty of salmon with the people. In tree after tree they can be heard grumbling over the weather, gossiping over the ravens, calling their rights to one another. They brush their wings against the heavy air; they cluck and peck and sway on the branches of the evergreen trees from which they eye one another and the salmon. What bounty, they must think. What bounty, the people think.

Who loves this land better, the eagles, the ravens, or the people? How can they be separated from one another? How can they be separated from the land?

The bear is in her den. Though it is now daytime, she sleeps. Beside her, the cubs stir and dream. Outside, the snow on the mountains is deep. White. Everything is covered with snow. She also dreams. She dreams of men and of distant places and of the stalks of certain grasses. She dreams of salmon.

Under the bright frozen water, the eggs are sleeping too. Slowly their yolk sacs grow. Slowly the eggs become adhesive and oily in the hardening water. Slowly the new salmon grow. On one bright sunlit day, while the bear still sleeps, the salmon larvae gather the strength to burst from their egg state, sharp teeth ready. At once, the salmon burrow into the gravel. They wait. They absorb their egg sacs, they grow stronger, and they wait.

When the sac has given all of itself and no more nourishment can be found, the salmon join the water column and search for food more substantial. In the bright sunlight, they gather to migrate downstream, to approach the estuary, to hunt and to be hunted. In the estuary they gather to eat and to be eaten, to allow their changing bodies to be received by the salt water that calls them. They gather there, and those that survive enter the salt water until that day they are called back.

Somewhere in the deep ocean, they will grow and will mature and they will strengthen. They will go into seaward waters so deep that even though it is daytime, there are still dark and dangerous places. They will live there. They will be absent and incomplete there. One day it will be time for them to go home, and they will gather. They will finally be called home. Called by the bear and by the people. Called by the land.

My first few years back home in Juneau brought relief and happiness as well as loss and harm. I sobered up. My mother died. I became a grandmother. I returned to school. A relationship ended. When I was offered a seagoing position on the M/V *Wilderness Discoverer*, it sounded like a summer of freedom and adventure.

Every five days, the small cruise ship loaded up tourists and embarked on its scheduled route. After a day of preparation, we departed Juneau in the early evening. After introductions, some of the crew accompanied the passengers to the observation deck, getting to know them, pointing out sights, and enjoying with them the beginning of a new trip. We steamed south on Gastineau Channel. I pointed out the ruins of the Alaska-Juneau gold mine, where I had climbed and run as a child. Mt. Juneau towering behind us, we entered Stephens Passage. We rounded Douglas Island, heading for Lynn Canal and Skagway in the morning. The steep Coast Mountains and Chilkat Mountains surrounded us. On clear days, the air sparkled at the tops of the mountains, reflected in the calm water.

At dawn on the first full day we arrived in Skagway, an ancient name meaning weather-beaten place, for the constant north wind. After a morning on the White Pass Yukon Railway, climbing to the frozen pass in a turn-of-the-century boxcar threading its way through tunnels and over trails built in a frenzy for gold, we rushed back to the boat and continued south the short distance to Haines. The original name of that historic town is Deishú. End of the trail. A guided tour took us to the Chilkat River, where we were sure to see brown bear, mountain goats, eagles, and jumping salmon. Then to a salmon bake situated at old Fort Seward, amidst a clan house furnished with carved house posts and surrounded by totems. At the end of the day, we headed south again for Glacier Bay, southbound again, the setting sun before us, the Chilkat Mountains at our side, the long summer day inviting us back to the observation deck to enjoy the evening sights of whales and porpoise playing in our wake.

At sunrise, we picked up a park ranger in Bartlett Cove at the entrance to Glacier Bay and steamed for Tarr Inlet, where the confluence of the Tarr and Margerie glaciers provided sights of calving glaciers, lazy seals, excited gulls.

Glacier Bay is an ancestral home of the Lingít people. It holds the hearts of the original people of this land. Now it is called Sít' Eeti Geey—the place where the glacier was. I fell in love on my trips to Glacier Bay that summer. It was the same experience that I had had when falling in love at any other time: my heart was tender and beat a little faster when I thought of Glacier Bay, I smiled at thoughts of the place. My eyes longed for the sights I would see there.

We enjoyed lunch while we lingered at the confluence of the glaciers at the top of Glacier Bay, watching for the glaciers to calve. From inland on the glacier we heard loud murmurs and sudden noises. The glacier talking to us. The calving caused loud noises called white thunder, frightening the gulls and causing waves that rhythmically rocked our boat. Seals held to the icebergs or slipped into the water while gulls waited for their chance to pick riches from amid the abandoned bergs.

After a day in Glacier Bay, we awoke at Point Adolphus, a favorite feeding spot for humpback whales. Their majestic presence overwhelmed all of us every time they drew near. Cries of joy and gasps of astonishment erupted from ecstatic passengers charmed by their power. After a day of cruising we arrived in Sitka, where a winding walk through Totem Park calmed us and reminded us that the place was accustomed to an ancient culture. Then a day of sailing through Peril Straits while passengers re-packed luggage and traded addresses with new friends.

Early on the final morning, we rounded Douglas Island and were treated to the sight of Juneau ahead, nestled at the foot of the mountains. There was never a more beautiful sight, in that summer filled with snow-capped mountains, glistening waters, humpback whales, and glaciers, than the view from the topmost deck: coming home.

North toward Chilkat. Chilkat Mountains on one side, Coast Mountains on the other. We are leaving Aak'w territory and entering Chilkoot territory, going past Berner's Bay. Daxanáak.

Not long ago, the Lingít marked their boundaries primarily with bodies of water. Berner's Bay, originally called Daxanáak, was well known for berries and good fishing. It was the acknowledged dividing line between the Chilkat Kwan and the Auk Kwan. Daxanáak lies within the ancestral territory of the Auk Kwan. It is still remembered for the richness of its fish and the abundance of its berries.

Past Eldred Rock, where rhubarb grows in winter daylight. From here we can see the Chilkat Islands. Not far from here is Deishú. And Skagway. Shgagwéi. Weather-Beaten Place.

Lingít place-names describe characteristics of the land or important events that took place there. Shgagwéi can be said to mean weather-beaten place, or place worn by the north wind. It is not often thought of as an ancient Native site. Modern Skagway presents itself as an 1890s gold rush town and is the major northern terminus for most of the cruise ships that visit Alaska. Yet its history of Native use and occupation is as rich and sure as all the other parts of Southeast Alaska. It was the revelation of gold in northern areas that delivered the killing blow to Lingít cultural ties to the land. It was only then that trade routes held by the Chilkat and Chilkoot people for generations were finally captured, for not even their fierce belief in justice could stem the tide of greed for land and gold.

Within the last few years, the Native people of Skagway, few in number, have formed a traditional council and have begun to make themselves known. Their presence has surprised some and inspired others.

Heading south again, the marine path passes Haines. The original name for Haines is *Deishú*, meaning end of the trail. Haines is within the ancestral territory of the Chilkoot people. It is not far from the ancient village of Klukwan, in Chilkat territory, where my grandfather's people still live. The old trails once led from village to village, along the water and into the interior. Songs and stories once passed along those old trails.

South toward Sitka way. Passing Favorite Channel. Killer whales jumped over us there.

I worked as a naturalist for a whale watching outfit one summer. Several times each day I met a vanload of twenty tourists and single-filed them down the ramp to a waiting jet boat. As soon as we left the no-wake zone of the inner harbor, we sped northwest toward Point Retreat. It was my job to spot whales, looking for the telltale column of vapor in the distance that revealed the presence of a humpback whale.

We weren't always lucky. On this day, anxious passengers and an even more anxious captain poured waves of tension over me while I watched the water, bracing myself on the back deck and scanning the horizon with binoculars. When we weren't lucky enough to find a whale, the captain turned the boat toward the east shore of Shelter Island—Favorite Channel, the long way back. I spied a spout at the north tip of Shelter. We stopped to watch a couple of humpbacks. The passengers were satisfied. It was time to head back to Auke Bay. Halfway down Favorite Channel, I spotted killer whales. The column of vaporous breath—the blow—from a killer whale is shorter than from a humpback and points forward, compared to the humpback's vertical spout. Killer whales are more rare. Killer whales are unpredictable. Killer whales don't stay long in one place.

We slowed the boat to an idle, well away from the whales. It looked like an acrobatic pod of about seven females. They jumped and splashed and raced. They sped straight toward us, dipping under the boat at the last minute, paying us no attention. Neither the captain nor I had ever seen killer whales move so fast or come so close. Two killer whales accompanied by a small juvenile splashed only a few yards from the boat. One of them threw something into the air. It spun and spiraled; the mature female caught it and threw it again while the young killer whale nosed it. The next time she threw it in the air, I recognized the shape of a spinning baby seal. The killer whales were teaching their young one to hunt. They played with the seal in the manner that a cat plays with a mouse. Jubilation turned to understanding. We were watching deadly play. Killer whales jumped over us there.

Saginaw Channel. Barlow Cove. Point Retreat in the setting sun. Here is the place where humpback whales bubblenetted in the fall. This is the place where we were surrounded by killer whales. We are leaving Aak'w territory and entering Xutsnoowú territory. Xutsnoowú. Fortress of the Bear. Stronghold of the Deisheetaan.

Fifteen years after United States men at Sitka negotiated a transaction with Russian men that resulted in the loss of millions of acres of ancient occupied lands, and only six years after the famous military engagement at Little Bighorn, an important shaman died aboard a white-owned whaling vessel when a whaling gun exploded. Following Lingít custom, men stopped work to bring ashore the boat containing the body and requested compensation of two hundred blankets. The owner of the whaling station reported to military authorities that his boat had been seized and two men taken hostage. The Navy commander brought a civilian barge and a revenue cutter to the village. The commander demanded that the people of Angoon pay him four hundred blankets.

The name Xutsnoowú means fortress of the bear—the place now known as Admiralty Island is said to have the largest concentration of brown bears in the world. The brown bear is a main crest of a number of Eagle clans. Admiralty Island, the main stronghold of the brown bear, is also the main stronghold of the Deisheetaan people, a Raven clan whose main crest is the Beaver. The Native people of Angoon were unable to assemble four hundred blankets in one day. The commander warned them that he would bombard the village if payment were not obtained and raised his demand to eight hundred blankets.

During all that day and into the following night, the people salvaged food and clan belongings. On October 26, the commander shelled the village and sent men ashore to burn Angoon and destroy the canoes. The people who died included six Native children. Homes and storehouses were burned down. Everything left in the houses, including winter stores of food and family heirlooms, was lost. One canoe—a Beaver canoe not at the village when it was bombed—survived. That canoe saved the people. It was used for fishing, gathering, and hunting to help get through the winter. It was with the help of that Beaver canoe that the village endured.

The prow of the canoe, an important clan emblem, was traditionally removed from the boat when it was in use. The carved Beaver figure disappeared in 1910 and turned up in 1911 in New York City as part of a collection of George Emmons, a man who had served under the commander who bombarded the village. The payment Emmons received for the cherished heirloom is said to have been forty-five dollars. The Beaver Prow lay unidentified in the New York museum until 1999, when a man from Angoon visited the museum. Although the prow was covered by other objects, he heard the Beaver Prow call to him.

In September of that year, the Beaver Prow came back to Alaska. Elders of the village, whose uncles and fathers and grandfathers had never let them forget the Beaver canoe, welcomed it home with glad words and fitting ceremony. We can be sure that the brown bear also welcomed it home.

Peril Strait. Dead Man's Reach. We are leaving Xutsnoowú territory and entering Sheet'ká territory. Poison Cove. Place where a brown bear and her two cubs watched us. Sergius Narrows. Salisbury Sound. Neva Strait. Place where brown bears browsed for grass. Highwater Island. Place where the Kaagwaantaan once came for berries. Old Sitka. Back to the place where you see Angoon again. Chatham Strait. Here we pass through Kuiu territory and enter Shtax' héen territory. Here is a place called Bitter water. Here is the place that calls itself Little Norway.

The town now called Petersburg was given that title to memorialize a man of Norwegian descent by the name of Peter Bushmann. Like many European and American men, Bushmann had quickly recognized the wealth to be gained from the rich waters of Southeast Alaska. Nearby Le Conte Glacier, named in the nineteenth century after a California geologist, provided ice with which to keep salmon fresh. In the late 1800s, Bushmann built a fishing fleet and invited friends and family to the area. By the mid-twentieth century, the town now known as Petersburg enjoyed the wealthiest per-capita income in Southeast Alaska as well as the largest and best-kept fishing fleet. Everybody in town now celebrates an annual Little Norway festival, when they wear *bunads* and eat lutefisk.

Native occupation in this area was almost as ignored as was Skagway's original population. But Petersburg has taken measures to restore that old history. Pamphlets feature ancient petroglyphs and fish traps found on a Petersburg beach. Plans are in place to erect two totem poles, the first in recent memory. Since totem poles are among the top attractions in most other Southeast Alaska towns, Petersburg tardily joining the bandwagon is presumably better than no bandwagon at all. Not yet erected, the poles lie on a lawn in downtown Petersburg, not far from the scaffolded Viking sailing ship taken down now and then for a Little Norway parade.

A few miles south of Petersburg on Mitkof Island is a trail that cuts through a coniferous forest that is home to the oldest spruce and hemlock trees in this area. Next to this old growth forest is a muskeg. The boardwalk trail winds through the muskeg a foot or two above the soggy ground. The day hangs wet above our footsteps. The forest and muskeg have lived here longer than the residents of Little Norway. They have lived here longer than the carvers of the poles and longer than the petroglyphs. The forest and muskeg along Ohmer Creek Trail counsel us all to endure.

Wrangell Narrows at midnight. Sumner Strait. Wrangell. A summertime trip on the Stikine River Flats. Stikine Strait. We pass through Kasaan territory and enter Tongass territory. Prince of Wales Island. Tongass Narrows. Ketchikan.

When I came back home I had enough of a bankroll to get as far as the first Alaska port. With a companion I'd met along the way, I left Seattle on the Alaska state ferry, my dog locked in a container on the car deck thinking she'd died and gone to dog hell. I slept in the solarium and visited her during twice-daily car deck calls. When we made it to Ketchikan, my companion and I found a place a few hundred yards south of downtown and set up a camp in the trees. We camped there for three months and then, after we were told to move, we set up camp at the Deer Mountain trailhead.

Each day my dog and I walked into town to visit the Seamen's Center and the Salvation Army food line. Late in the summer, huckleberries lined the trail down the mountain. Often I climbed the rocks to fill bags with plump red berries to take to the Seamen's Center and trade for coffee or a shower. Sometimes I picked berries behind Tatsuda's Grocery Store, where huckleberries covered a rocky hill dotted with footpaths and places to sit in the hot sun. I munched on berries and watched my dog run and play. Sometimes we made a fishing line out of string and caught rockfish off the dock. We carried the fish back to camp, roasted it on a handmade grill, and feasted on fresh rockfish, handout bread, and huckleberries. At the end of the summer, I got a job and a place to stay and sent for my mother. Two years later, we all made it all the way back to Juneau.

Years later, training for a naturalist position aboard the state ferry, I took the ferry to Prince of Wales Island, climbed four hundred stairs up a steep mountainside, and crept into El Capitan Cave, the largest known cave in Alaska. In this and other caves, remains of animals, humans, tools, and weapons have been uncovered that are so ancient — greater than forty thousand years for brown and black bear, ten thousand years for human remains and tools — they have caused scientists to rewrite their favorite theories. I would have liked to sit quietly in the dark almost-silence, hearing only the ancient trickle of time as the rain forest water slowly carved these massive caves, drop by patient drop. I would have liked to feel the cave close its breath and embrace me in the generations of this land. I would have liked to imagine myself lost in this cave, hearing a woman's moan or smelling the nearness of a bear. I would have liked to be alone.

Instead, the guide flicked off his flashlight and in an uninterrupted monologue admonished the group to appreciate the silence. After a few moments, he turned his lamp back on and guided us across sharp rocks and along smooth walls, leading us over deep caverns, avoiding a maze of other paths, to the entrance, where we blinked in surprise at the daylight.

Oral history, too often the object of dismissive scientific sensibility, has proven itself to be true in more than one case when chronicling the conduct of glaciers. In the part of Southeast Alaska now called by the name Glacier Bay, an old story tells of the advance of a glacier with such rapid movement that the water churned before it. Long discounted by scholars, this phenomenon has now been observed, notably by scientists studying the rapid advance of Le Conte Glacier in 1998, when observers recorded the glacier's noisy advance into the agitated waters before it.

Oral history now almost lost teaches that certain old clans followed the melting ice down main rivers into what is now Southeast Alaska. When those people arrived at this place, old stories say, they found people already living here. Oral history asserts and elders affirm that people have lived on these ancestral lands since time immemorial. Although the phrase doesn't comfortably rest within Western parameters, it has long been understood by Native people to mean many thousands of years. Others, however, developed theories that denied human occupation during certain ice age periods and placed a lesser estimate on the length of human habitation in Southeast Alaska. These theories are being rewritten now that the caves on Prince of Wales Island have revealed that even during the last of the Wisconsin Ice Age, dated to some nine thousand years ago, refugia supported life along a wide strip of habitable land on this and other islands of Southeast Alaska. Current scientific discoveries suggest that this rich land has continuously provided sustenance to the people and animals that have belonged here since time immemorial.

Revillagegedo Channel. Annette Island. Leaving Lingít territory. Entering Haida territory. Dixon Entrance.

After twenty-five years' absence, I finally made it home. I boarded an Alaska state ferry in Seattle on a cloudy-at-last day, made myself comfortable in the solarium, and spent all my time watching the water as the vessel carried us northward at its fifteen-knot pace. I woke at dawn on Mother's Day, May 10, 1986, and walked to the railing on the upper deck. The humming engines became the sound of Dixon Entrance, a wide passage named after an eighteenth-century crewmember of James Cook. Something was different in the sky. Something was different on the water. The open sea to the west signaled our position: we were crossing the international boundary between Canada and Alaska. We were entering Lingít Aaní. I was home.

As a deckhand on a jet boat taking visitors on two-hour whale watching tours, the next summer was filled with rushing, always at the beck and call of captains, owners, staff, and tourists. I met each load of passengers delivered to the dock by the company bus, walked them down the ramp, and helped them board the red jet boat. "Watch your step, please. Make yourself comfortable. Watch your head stepping down. Watch your step, please. Make yourself comfortable." One after the other. Time after time.

With everyone seated, I untied the boat and cast off at the captain's pleasure. Usually he was in a hurry: impatient, concerned about every minute, mindful that we were scheduled to return in exactly two hours for another load of tourists. Sometimes, though, he gabbed on the radio or visited the head or compared notes with captains on other boats while I stood smiling, rope in hand, waiting for his signal to cast off.

We left the harbor, motoring slowly through the no-wake zone. I stowed the bumpers, closed the hatches, and grabbed an orange Mae West life vest for the requisite safety talk. I pointed out the fire extinguishers and flare kit, demonstrated the floating device, and cautioned everyone to remain seated when the boat was in motion. Children fussed and passengers chatted.

"Humpback whales from the greater Juneau vicinity are known to winter in Hawaii, where they breed and give birth but do not feed," I repeated to a new group every two hours. "They return to our rich waters here in Alaska, where they feed on krill, herring, and other small schooling fish. They eat a ton or more a day, every chance they get. Sometimes it seems like they're eating all the time." I paused here to glance at the boat's progress, timing my speech with the buoy marker past which we could try our luck at accelerating, not always a sure thing. "Captain says that's what it's like to be on a tour ship." Pausing also gave me a sense of the group — the more they laughed at my first joke, the better the crowd.

"The mountains around Juneau are only three to five thousand feet in elevation, but they appear much higher because they're so steep," I bragged. "Picture that many of these islands are just as steep as the mountains, so the water is quite deep even close to the land." I gestured toward the coastline. "Remember we're looking for a column of vapor. Be sure to look right up against the islands, because there might be a whale where we would normally consider the shore." I looked around again. "It's a beautiful day in the rain forest!" I exclaimed, no matter what the weather. "Let's go whale watching!"

I held my breath, hoping that the captain would synchronize the boat's acceleration with the end of my talk. And when he did, the captain and I would both hold our breath and hope that the boat would speed over the water, instead of dragging itself along, jets clogged, plugs misfiring, r.p.m. on the starboard engine only half what it was on the port side, while I stood smiling, bagels and juice in hand, offering refreshments to visitors who had paid good money to see whales, and by god they expected to see them.

"They told us not to let you go more than two hours without giving you something to eat!" I shouted over the jets, pausing again for laughter. The boat bounced and lurched on the waves while I braced myself and balanced a platter of twenty bagels and twenty pouches of juice, waiting for some matron from Florida to decide just exactly which bagel she really wanted (*They're all the same! Take one!*) and for her husband to decipher what a dadgummed pouch was — a bag of juice? Never heard of it. Juice? You sure this is juice? (*Yes! It's juice! Take one! Or not, I don't care! Just make up your mind! Please! I beg you!*)

"On the port side in the far distance is Admiralty Island," I continued. "The original name for that island is Xutsnoowú, which means 'Fortress of the Brown Bear.' That's a good name for it, because the brown bear population on that large island is thought to be one bear per square mile. At sixteen hundred square miles, it's the largest concentration of brown bear in the world." Another pause while I held up my hands to show my silver bracelets. "The Native people of this area associate themselves with different animals that we then take as our crests. My clan—the Wolf clan—considers itself related to the brown bear, so I'm always careful to point it out to you when we go by!" For some reason, this never failed to make them laugh.

"When I was a girl, my grandmother used to tell me we don't eat brown bear meat, because to do so would be just like eating our own cousin!" The captain had been surprised when he realized that I still considered the brown bear my cousin, the Taku Wind my grandfather, the spider my neighbor. After being brought the truths of virgin birth, resurrection, and walking on water, why would I now persist in believing a myth? But I let the passengers laugh, the captain preach, the jet engines clog. Every day is the same, every passenger is the same. Every captain is the same. Every moment is unique.

Just outside Barlow Cove, a dozen humpback whales have surrounded a school of herring in the deep ocean water. Beneath the water, one circles a spiral net of bubbles around the fish. The whale constructs the net of bubbles upward from the floor of the ocean, trapping the herring in smaller and smaller circles, nearer and nearer the surface. Then one humpback begins to circle the net and the trapped herring, singing in a high-pitched haunting voice, frightening the herring into a huddled ball of prey that rises to the top.

We hear the song over a hydrophone that the captain has lowered into the water. We look in every direction, searching for telltale bubbles. Eagles and gulls fly overhead, circling, calling, searching. I watch the gulls. They will know before I do where the whales will come up. "There! Over there!" A dozen whales lunge out of the water, mouths open, pink tongues and baleen and splashing water, gulls diving, passengers gasping, hearts racing.

Then they are gone. Back under the water, checking for herring, swallowing their last mouthfuls, yumming their dinner. They surface again, slow and graceful; their breath explodes and their spouts are a loud wet sticky whoosh; they are so close to us, powerful, graceful, gentle. Oblivious to our presence.

The whales begin to travel away from us, into Barlow Cove chasing herring; we all want to go with them, but the captain has something else in mind. "Be seated, please. The captain wants us to be seated, he has something else to show us. Be seated, please." In a flurry of joy and disappointment, thrills and complaints, the passengers are seated, I close the hatches, the jets roar and we're off, steaming toward False Point.

We no sooner round Point Retreat than we are in the midst of two dozen or more boats: whale watchers, sport fishing craft, commercial fishing vessels, private motorized skiffs. The late sun reflects off the almost calm waters of Lynn Canal. The lighthouse at Point Retreat catches a ray of late afternoon sun, Eagle Glacier glistening on the mainland behind it. The beautiful Chilkat Mountains are capped in white and shrouded in summer-evening patchy clouds. The captain slows the boat, I open the doors to the decks, we pile out onto the aft deck. All around the boats spread up and down the waterway are the dorsal fins of killer whales. There must be more than fifty. More than sixty. In the reflected sun, their fins are dark against the water, black signals rising from the water, moving fast and disappearing, running in the water. Wolves of the sea.

"It's very rare to see both killer whales and humpbacks on the same trip," I point out to the passengers, "especially humpbacks that are bubble-net feeding, and especially so many killer whales. We're very fortunate." The passengers are in awe; only a few of them are not yet satisfied, but those are the passengers who will never be happy; if nothing else, they'll complain about the bagels. Most of the passengers are thrilled to silence, beside themselves with joy. They realize what I'm saying is the truth. This is a rare trip. This is a rare moment.

The air becomes still. We become quiet. Together, we witness a sight few people ever see. We are surrounded by killer whales. We are surrounded by freedom.

Conventional teachings of the captain and the day suggest that eternity is something that starts after death, and then goes on—well, forever. But I know that it is this moment that is eternal. One wave moves in one certain manner while that particular killer whale rises above the water and catches one ray of light against the flash of its singular fin, and I stand here on this particular boat, late in the afternoon of this certain day, with these people who have traveled distances near and far to stand here and be captured with me in this moment, which is gone before I blink and which will continue always to exist.

The captain gives the signal to be seated for our long return trip to the dock, where we will offload these passengers, refuel and clean the boat, radio the dispatcher for tomorrow's schedule, and be finished with our work for this day. I will limp home, feet sore, tired, hungry, sick of bagels, wash the salt water out of my hair, lie down on the couch, talk on the phone, fall asleep. I will rise the next day to work again until the summer ends, and then I will return to the university where I am belatedly completing my education. I will see more whales and eagles, I will see rough weather and calm. I will grow older, I will grow old. I will die. And all the while, a part of me will be lost in one moment, killer whales will surround me forever, that eternal moment will never happen again.

A man I knew told stories. He was one of those people who carries on conversations in Lingít. One Sunday morning as we sat over beers down at the Arctic Bar, he told me about his uncle.

"My uncle went berrypicking with two of his brothers. They made noise and talked out loud, but they had no weapons. After a while he wandered away quite a bit, following heavy bushes. He pulled down one bush to look behind it and right in front of his face there was a big brown bear staring at him." My friend gestured and made a face to illustrate his story.

A distinction is made between brown bears and black bears. Black bears are seen around garbage dumps or poking around houses in the backyard. Signs on the public buses show a crossed-out silhouette of a bear in a garbage can. Their caption reads Garbage Kills Bears. There are strict laws about securing household garbage. Once or twice every summer day there are bear calls to the police. It is almost always a black bear.

Brown bears are larger, more unpredictable, more dangerous. They are more truly our cousins. They are the bears that can most easily kill. Not always acknowledging our relationship, they will eat us if they think we might taste good. They're attracted more to berries and to salmon than to garbage. They stay in wilder places.

"My uncle never flinched," my friend continued. "He just stood there. They had a staring contest, one face only a few feet in front of the other. He said it went on for five or ten minutes. My uncle never moved.

"The bear never moved either. The two of them just stared at each other. Pretty soon the bear turned around real fast, walked away a little bit, and turned around and charged him. It stopped right in front of my uncle's face again and stared at him. My uncle never flinched."

This same man when a boy had crawled across a fallen log over a creek to reach a place where he could catch dog salmon. The water was thick with fish. There were three boys, carrying empty baskets on their backs. They jumped off the log, ran down to the creek and began gaffing salmon, throwing the fish over their backs, not looking behind them. In only minutes they knew they had enough for the first load to carry proudly over the log back to the village. They turned to load the fish in their baskets and there was a black bear helping itself to their fish, not paying any attention to them at all. In alarm they sprinted to the log, the smallest boy hollering "Wait! Wait!" as they ran.

They crawled across the log as fast as they could, the small boy now hollering "Hurry! Hurry!" as they crawled. The bear, obviously an old sow well used to the antics of young ones, never even looked at them. This small boy was the uncle of whom my friend now spoke.

"He never flinched," the story continued. "Three times the bear charged him. Three times the bear ran right up to the bush my uncle was holding. Three times my uncle just stood there. Strong. The fourth time the bear finally went away." We tipped our beer in salute to his brave uncle.

One time a man was lost in the fog in a skiff. The family went fishing and everybody came back but him. His brothers and cousins got together and after talking for a while they decided that everyone would go back out and look for him. This man's uncle was the one who found him, tied up at the light buoy. The man was so happy to be rescued he started crying when he saw the boat coming. When his uncle stepped into the skiff to embrace him, his crying nephew took hold of his hand and bit it hard.

The man's uncle jerked his hand away. "Why did you do that?"

"I thought you were a Kóoshdaa Káa!" the nephew sobbed.

A long time ago, it is said, Lingít people were fair skinned, with deep auburn-colored hair. I remember a man just like that. I used to see him around town when I was a girl. His name was Indian Red.

One time, Indian Red decided to climb over two mountains and hunt for mountain goat. It was possible to go to the first mountain and get grouse, but a good hunter needed to go to the second mountain to get goat. Indian Red started out right before dawn. When he finally got to the second mountain, he shot his goat and packed it all up to put on his shoulders. Then he started walking. He knew it would be dark long before he made it back. The sun went down. He kept walking. Even when he was tired, he didn't stop. He kept walking. He got over one mountain and was on his way up the last one. He had to stop for a while. After he put down his pack and took a long piss, he sat down for a minute and lit up a cigarette. A Chesterfield. Pretty soon up walked a Kóoshdaa Káa. It looked just like his younger brother.

"You made it!" the Kóoshdaa Káa said. "We were worried about you!"

Indian Red put out his cigarette and said, "I only stopped here for a minute. I'm on my way home. Let's go."

The Kóoshdaa Káa walked in front, and Indian Red thought it best to go along. Indian Red stopped. The Kóoshdaa Káa stopped, too, and Indian Red said to him, "Why don't you carry this for a while, that way we'll get home quicker."

The Kóoshdaa Káa picked up the pack. Pretty soon the sun came up. They kept walking. Next thing Red knew, the sun was going down again. It seemed like they had walked all day. The Kóoshdaa Káa had to stop, it was such a heavy pack. The Kóoshdaa Káa said, "How much farther is it anyway?"

"It's a long way yet," Indian Red told him. In fact it was just around the corner.

When he heard that, the Kóoshdaa Káa threw the pack on the ground and walked away. That's how Indian Red tricked a Kóoshdaa Káa.

I often began my girlish adventures by running to the local cemetery, dashing uphill on Capitol Avenue from our old house where it unbuckled at the edge of the village. During the day, I headed for the trails on the north side of Mt. Juneau, or up the south side of the mountain to play in the fast-running water pouring down its steep slopes. But on a summer night, dusk at last falling, shadows finally lengthening, house lights now flickering on in streetside curtained windows, I headed with my grade-school chums to play hide-and-seek among the gravestones of Evergreen Cemetery, popping up in the shadows from behind the taller memories, laughing, shouting, whispering, the dearly departed no doubt resting in greater peace to the chorus of mischievous giggles.

My mother and grandmother showed me pictures and told me stories of the family dead who were buried in our plain plot in Evergreen Cemetery. The most tenderly mourned was my great-grandmother, Anna Willard—Kaadustéen. Ruth Willard Hayes—Saawdu.oo, my grandmother, Anna Willard's daughter—is buried near her now. An uncle, Benjamin—Lingít name unremembered—is there in a tiny homemade coffin, having died when only a year old. My favorite uncle, Ernest Hayes, Yaakwáan—Uncle Buzz—is also buried there, struck down by alcohol when he was only twenty-nine years old. My other uncles are buried in Sitka. I don't know when my grandfather died. I don't know where he was buried. The most recent to have joined her remains to the family plot is my mother, Erma Daisy Hayes—Kaaxkwéi—who died in my arms a few years ago. I expect my own ashes to be the next to nourish that wet ground near a shady tree, mine the next name to join the crowded memories of our family dead.

The community memories of Evergreen Cemetery fade with passing generations. A new cemetery out the road gives orderly rest to almost all of Juneau's newly deceased. There is no room in the new cemetery for crowded plots of which-way graves and private ashes. There are no headstones high enough for games of hide-and-seek.

The remains of Juneau's older memories are buried downtown. Many well-known Juneauites are at rest in the old Evergreen Cemetery. From the east, a strolling visitor first comes upon the well-tended graves of Joe Juneau and Richard Harris, the town's American founders. Joe Juneau died in the Klondike, his remains carried to Evergreen Cemetery in 1903; Harris died in Oregon and was buried in Evergreen Cemetery in 1907. Kaawa.ée, the Auk Tribe chief who is said to have guided Juneau and Harris to the gold that attracted so many people to the town, was cremated in 1892 in accordance with traditional Lingít practice; a bronze memorial to Kaawa.ée marks the western entrance to the cemetery. Chief Yaakwáan, brother to my great-grandmother Anna Willard, is buried near Kaawa.ée. Yaakwáan's grave, headstone broken and almost unreadable, lies on the edge of a small rise at the corner of the graveyard. A path near it is a shortcut for students from the nearby high school who rush to secluded places under the trees, ignoring the scolding ravens. The students are anxious for a few private moments among the graves. Not many years ago, they may have played hide-and-seek.

Evergreen Cemetery, established in 1890, was not the first American-sanctioned cemetery in Juneau. The original graveyard was located on a hillside now called Chicken Ridge, at the top of Main Street. In 1887, a mining claim was recorded at the site of that original graveyard; most, but not all, of the graves were removed from the old site by 1892. The mining patent was never used for a claim. The ptarmigan for which the area is said to have been named have disappeared. The ravens have moved with the dead to the Evergreen graves.

By 1914, the land at the old cemetery had been divided into lots. The area was becoming known as a fine location for some of the more expensive new homes of the growing town. The old cemetery was cleared to make room for new homes. Juneau's Native people learned that the graves of their loved ones were being dug up and exhumed bodies thrown over the east side of the hill along with the excavated dirt. Small coffins and large were shoved over the side of the hill. Bones were scattered, a piece of scalp with long brown hair still clinging was found near the foundation of one of the new houses. Relatives of the dead complained to a local Presbyterian missionary and to an official of the Interior Office Land Department. The group making these complaints included Harry Phillips, Jimmie Young, Fannie Rudolph, Mr. and Mrs. Jack Yaakwaan, and my great-grandmother, Annie Willard.

The original people traditionally cremated their dead, sending along personal effects to ease the coming journey, and burning favorite foods from time to time to satisfy appetites not subdued by death. But the practice of cremation was seen as crude and un-Christian by the missionaries who came early to save souls and to obliterate heathen customs; enforcing the European custom of burying the bones and flesh and topping it off with a stone to hold down the spirit was an important part of preaching Indian spiritual conversion. The irony was not lost on missionary James Condit, who observed that Natives accepted scriptural teaching, adopted consecrated burial, and then along came white men to dig up their bodies and throw the bones over the side of a hill.

Among the desecrated bodies listed in Condit's 1914 letter of Presbyterian protest was that of Anna Willard's cousin, Wanya, whose remains were identified among the debris. A relation of Chief Johnson was identified by the handmade blanket buried with him; three children named Jackson were recognized by the playthings buried with them and by the bottle of medicine sent against future harm. One unearthed body was said to be Benjamin Shotridge, a man important to the Presbytery, recognized by his burial clothes: two blankets, a pair of slippers, his trousers, a decorated glove. His leather shoes. Somebody found a mitten with part of a hand still inside, but no one could be sure whose flesh still gripped the beaded cloth.

When he received a letter of complaint from Special Agent Lewis, Commissioner Marshall concluded there was no real actionable offense, since the cemetery was now on private land and therefore outside federal jurisdiction. That the land had been dishonestly taken in the first place was not part of the discussion.

In his letter, Lewis described a visit by a Native woman who asked if she and her husband could enter that private land to remove the remains of a relative before the grave was destroyed. A land-owning attorney granted permission on behalf of the other title holders, but the next day the woman found no trace of her relative's grave. She returned to Lewis's office in tears. When he explained to her that the people excavating the old cemetery owned a patent to the land, she asked, "What right has the government to give patent to land where our people are buried? Has a patent been given for the bodies of our friends? White men crowd Natives out from the land on which their very homes stand. Will they not even allow our dead to have a resting place?" The answer to this, if one was provided, was never recorded.

A halfhearted action was brought in federal court. Lists of buried Natives were placed in evidence, outraged Presbyterians called to provide testimony, bereaved Natives subpoenaed from their fish camps. Officially appointed men debated jurisdiction and argued easement. Nothing came of the action. Most of the remaining graves were moved to the new Evergreen Cemetery; loved ones whose bodies could not be found tumbled down the slope of the hill or piled in the excavated dirt were mourned for a time and then forgotten.

In the summer there is the smell of new-cut grass. Songbirds sing and distant dogs bark. Only rarely are human voices heard, calling in the distance, waking the living from their summer reveries. In the winter, when the ground is cold and frozen, I'm glad that my mother was cremated, for I would worry at the cold had she not been. In the winter, the silence of graveyards and the chill of death surround all the graves. A few stubborn ravens rest nearby. They don't waste their energy calling. They are mostly silent, like the graves. They are mostly hungry, like the dead. They wait for spring.

Years ago, when I lived in California, it was my practice to keep my sons home from school on the first day of spring. I cooked a turkey dinner; I planned the summer garden and gave small gifts. Now, sons grown, my

Spring Day celebrations are modest: no turkey dinners, no seed packets for elaborate summer gardens of tomatoes and squash. No robins or mocking-birds in the trees building nests and collecting twigs. No dread of hot weather. No gifts. My spring observance now involves a visit with my grandson to Evergreen Cemetery to tidy up the family plot. We tend my mother's grave and the graves of my grandmother and great-grandmother. I don't know if Wanya's grave was eventually reclaimed, and if so, if it lies here or with Chief Yaakwáan, buried farther away. But the ravens know. This is the place where winter was.

My grandson and I neaten up. We replace flowers on the stones. Even on bright mornings, our family's patch of earth is shady. There are dots of color here and there on our plot and throughout the cemetery, where flowers and ribbons and memories decorate the graves. Tears drip from my nose and join the solid snow. Generations are crowded into this small patch of land, where our dead have for a time been allowed their resting place.

We will return home and light a fire in the woodstove. I will brew tea and think about the return of spring. I'll miss my mother. I'll plant a kiss on my grandson's cheek. Although he never knew my mother, he'll talk about how much he misses her. In his innocence, he will personify spring. He will persuade me to the hope of life renewed.

When my mother and I first left Alaska, she planned to send for her mother as soon as she could. But she received a letter from her younger sister Rusty, telling her that my grandmother had died. Holding the letter, my mother burst into uncontrolled tears, bending over with unman-ageable wracking sobs, while I marveled at the sight of my stoical mother collapsing in grief.

In the Lingít culture, mourning transcends the individual. A funda-mental balance, manifested most profoundly in the balance between clans, is an essential component of the Lingít world view. When an individual dies, it is the clan that suffers the loss. The opposite clan carries out the preliminary ceremonies of death. After a time, the bereaved clan holds a payback party, making clear to the opposite clan the value of their words and acts of comfort. Thus balance is restored.

At the time that Washington men, or Boston men, came to Lingít Aaní, cremation was the custom. Only shamans were not cremated. Ashes were placed in mortuary poles or in bentwood boxes. Payback parties, called ƙu.éex', usually took place a year or so after the death. Presbyterianism, Catholicism, and Russian Orthodoxy had as important precepts the elimination of ancient practices and the adoption of Christian rituals in their place. One influence of Russian Orthodoxy in the Lingít culture is the observance of forty-day parties, a ritual not practiced before European contact, but now considered a central event in the mourning process. Few people are given a traditional memorial potlatch, for it is an expensive affair, but almost everyone has a forty-day party held in their honor, at which time it is counseled that tears should diminish, in order for the spirit to be freed.

It was my mother's way never to ask—for help, for gifts, for information. On a cloudy day in the first week of November, she called to let me know she was once again in the hospital. By that time, she had been losing weight for more than a year and weighed less than 75 pounds. It was not surprising for her to be hospitalized for observation and tests.

Her voice was weak and resigned: she was only reporting, she wasn't asking me for anything. She expected nothing. She wanted nothing. She knew I was busy, she said, she knew I had my own life. The doctor says I can't get up at all, she repeated. The doctor says I need to rest and it's too bad I don't have someone to help me. I don't know how I'll make it on my own.

I'll go with you, Mom, I told her. You know I'll help you.

My mother lived in a small corner apartment in a senior housing project in the middle of downtown Juneau. She had lived there alone ever since we'd finally returned to our hometown some years before. She'd never bought herself a new bedspread, nor placed a new rug on the bathroom floor, nor hung a picture on the wall. She sat in a corner by the window where I'd placed an old recliner years before. She read magazines and paperback novels most of the day, and smoked Pall Mall cigarettes. She glanced out the window to the busy center of the small town and at the old television in the other corner. She denied herself comforts. She would not pretty herself or her surroundings. She had no extra chairs for guests. She had no guests. She had no treats in the cupboard and no coffee on the stove. She sat in the corner, her perpetual frown creased deep on her face, giving me a big, welcoming smile when I visited. So little to offer.

Help yourself to instant coffee, sit down on the folding chair. Any plant or goldfish you bring to me will die. The stuffed animals you give me will be piled in a black plastic bag in the hall. I will not listen to the radio you buy for me. I will not eat the soufflé.

The doctor was surprised at my willingness to stay with my mother. Your mother said you were busy, the doctor told me. Your mother said she couldn't bother you. I stayed in the room while he examined her. Hello, Daisy! The doctor's cheerfulness was incongruous with my mother's silent frown. Let's see here! How's the blood pressure today? My mother's arm was smooth cool light brown skin over sharp bone. There was no flesh. My mother and I both looked away.

The doctor spoke in a loud voice, as if to a slow-witted child. Well! I see you've gained two pounds! You weigh seventy-two now! How do you feel, Daisy? Have you been eating?

My mother glared at the doctor, a thermometer gripped tight between grim lips. She frowned. Ahh, the doctor said and checked the thermometer. Why don't we let your daughter take you home! Bet you can't wait to be around your own things!

My mother's eyes flashed imperceptibly wider. Things—I forgot to get things! I need to go back, I need to live life all over again. I need to laugh and ask for help and smile! Things—I need things!

I stocked her cupboards and cleaned her bedroom and washed her bedding, brought her home in a chartered taxi, and made sense of the two dozen different sorts of pills sent with her. I slept on the floor in the living room since there was no couch. I didn't know what to do except hope that she would soon be well. One night less than a week after I brought her home she came out of the bedroom at midnight, dragging herself behind an aluminum walker, and told me to call 911. She couldn't breathe. Medics took her to the hospital, where she stayed for another few days. When she was released, the white-jacketed doctor made me understand that my mother would die.

My youngest son stayed in my home when I moved into my mother's apartment. Late in the afternoon of the winter solstice, he called to tell me that he had found my old dog Gypsy lying dead at the side of the road in front of the house. I sank to my knees in grief and in guilt. In answering my mother's needs I had abandoned my little companion. The next day, my partner, my son, a friend, and I wrapped Gypsy in a blanket, tossed in flowers, a bone, and a toy, and buried her on our property at the edge of the village.

My mother believed that now that she had finally quit smoking she would get well. She wanted only to live. She refused to sign a living will, telling me the doctor wanted to discuss it more with her, and telling the doctor that it was I who needed to talk more about it. When the doctor and I were both in the same room she said nothing at all.

She had a terror of the night. I gave her a spoon and aluminum pan to rattle when she needed me, sometimes every twenty minutes throughout the night. At the emergency room, she'd had a terrifying dream; darkness now frightened her and she needed reassurance from my constant presence. She felt the presence of her long-dead grandmother. She cried for my great-grandmother, whose death was an abandonment to her. Nevertheless she longed to live.

I prepared her meal trays temptingly, serving five small meals each day and other little snacks. My mother lay in the bed looking out the window, seeming not to see me preparing meals in the tiny kitchen directly in her line of sight, heating and spooning and toasting and pouring. When I brought the tray to her, she continued to look out the window until I called her.

Mom. I brought your food. Here's your pills. Mom. Mom. She would start as though surprised and wait for her bed to be adjusted. I asked her if the food looked good, did she want anything else, did she feel hungry.

It looks okay, my mother would weakly reply. No, she didn't want anything else. She wasn't really hungry. She never thanked me. She never smiled.

"Mom, do you remember when you were in the hospital when I was little? Do you remember before you were sent to Seward, when me and Grandma used to walk over to see you in the window?" I tucked the comforter around her chin. I checked under her thin bones and straightened the padding. I kissed her cool smooth forehead. "Mom? Do you remember?"

She looked out the window beside the bed. She smiled. "Yes." She opened her mouth, signaling for another taste of soup. The wet broth touched her hungry lips; she received a drop. "They took good care of me there. I was happy when you came to see me. I worried about you, there at the house, but I couldn't do anything about it." She turned away from the next spoonful of soup. "There was nothing I could do." She smoothed her cheek on the pillow as I stroked her hair. I glimpsed the slightest smile. She held my hand with cool thin fingers and pulled me forward to whisper in my ear. "Your father was the only man I ever loved."

She looked past my shoulder to a point that to me was only air. Did she know the deep effect it had on me not to be seen? Mom, I pleaded when I felt I needed badly to go outside. I have to go out for a while! I need to walk outside, I need fresh air. Please say something to me. Tell me it's okay.

A respite worker came twice a week. My mother retreated into silence when I made plans to go out for a few hours. But I knew she was as aware of me as if I were truly standing in the shaded place where my mother's eyes looked: palpable, touching her shoulder, beseeching. Do you want me not to go out, Mom? I asked. Just tell me. Just let me know.

Her spirit was always one of passive resistance: resignation, abdication, surrender. It was her purest strength, the sure knowledge that it is the helpless who will be carried. At her dying I saw the shadow of the deep and painful truth: I had within me the helpless surrender of my mother, and we both had within us not only the desire to be helpless, but the wish to be abandoned.

And at this final call, my mother, the symbol of strength, determination, indomitable will, became shamelessly weak, her careworn lovely face reaching oh so hesitantly with wrinkled lips toward the shaking spoon held gently to her dear face. Drink in this taste of broth! Slurp greedily and loudly the soup of life, of youth, of strength, of hope for life. Receive

into your mouth, your dry throat, your empty stomach, the tea of my sac-
rifice. Regain your strength, become young again, rise up, do not die! Do
not become a weak and helpless demanding babe. Be forever the strong,
the independent, the fierce mother of my youth!

My sons and I were called to Saint Ann's on the day after Easter. My
mother had entered the long-term hospital a few weeks before. By the
time we arrived, she couldn't speak. We gathered around her bed. Her eyes
were glazed, but when I took her in my arms, she turned her face toward
her only child and, above the mask of mortality closing over her face, sent
by the expression of her eyes one last weak smile. I held her in my arms
and hoped for life. One more night. One day, another chance. The light in
my mother's eyes was contrasted by a dark, unknowable, forbidden space.
A presence approached from the darkness behind her. My mother turned,
and turned again and motioned a goodbye. Not long later, she was gone.

On this first day of spring, I walk with my grandson to tend our family
graves. Footsteps crunching, I smooth packed snow over flat markers and
old plastic flowers, searching for a familiar name. As we walk, I entertain
him with stories of myself at his age. He concentrates, frowning at the
image of Grandma as a girl, paying careful attention. As though he knows
one day he will want to remember.

On the day before Christmas, my mother checked in to Saint Ann's Hospital, now a dreaded nursing home from which it was commonly believed
one never returned. On the day after Easter she died. She had always said
she wanted cremation, so I arranged for her body to be flown to Fairbanks.
When asked whether I wanted her ashes mailed to the mortuary or to
me, I couldn't allow either. I flew to Fairbanks and met a man at the air-
port who handed me a heavy little box containing the dense remains of
my mother. I held her ashes in my lap on the long flight back to Juneau.
　I placed my mother's ashes in a carved and painted bentwood box. The

memorial service was held in a private home. After the service, the box of ashes, her wallet, money, notes from her grandchildren and from me, and her favorite deerskin slippers were placed in the ground in the family plot in Evergreen Cemetery in Juneau, next to her mother, her brothers, and her grandmother. A Raven from the opposite side wiped the tears from our faces and eased handfuls of sodden dirt onto the balanced box in the small grave, while our Eagle family stood to the side, helpless and weeping.

It is not only the individual who mourns a lost loved one. It is not only the clan that feels the loss of an opposite. It is not only people or animals who are mourned, or who grieve. Even the land mourns the loss of her loved ones. There are mourning songs among the Lingít that sing of a pitiful land bereft of its people.

When you speak of a place, it is best also to talk about its history, of what that place means to the people who once there lived. Not to do so would be like picturing a lush and timeless woman, but choosing not to make mention of her lost children—those children to whom she gave fecund birth, whom she nourished at her rich fat breast, whom she loved no less than they loved her, who were seized and sent away from her arms, but whom she remembers and longs for every day. That is the same way that the land longs for her children. That is how pitiful the land is without her children.

A few weeks after her death, we held a forty-day party to release my mother's spirit. We served an abundance of traditional and modern foods; the Eagle/Raven dancers sang songs of celebration; everyone shared funny stories and memories. We burned plates of food so my mother and those with whom she now kept company could also hold a party. That night, my son watched northern lights flash through the sky. It is a rare sight in Southeast, especially in the summer. It told us that our mourning of death had been relieved by the celebration of life. It told us that balance had again been restored.

I touch the pink flesh of the just-fallen tree. Its smell. Its flesh. The softness of its flesh. The texture of its smooth pink flesh.

Gary and I walk up a hillside trail, skirting a few halfhearted mudslides, listening to the relieved singing of undecided birds, taking in the dappled sunlight. We've endured twelve inches of El Niño rain in twenty-four hours in the midst of the redwoods south of San Francisco. We've spent the night huddled together in a storage cabin perched on a steep hill listening to trees crash and slide. The radio has announced that a seven-county disaster area has been declared, but apart from impassable roads and houses covered and filled with mud, the worst is over.

A redwood tree is growing at a slant in the forest a few feet ahead, just off the path. "Is that tree growing that way?" I ask. As soon as I speak, the tree collapses, pulling and breaking branches and bushes in a reverberating crash that ends in headlong silence. We stand astounded for a few moments, then cautiously pick our way to the tree.

The trunk has snapped at about four feet. The jagged flesh of the tree is pink and thick. It looks as though it would be soft were I to touch it. I reach out a cautious hand and grip a handful of pink flesh. I bend down and place my cheek on the wound. Its smell is raw and moist. Not at all my idea of death.

"Saankaláxt'!" my grandmother called, and I always came running. She would send me on an errand, or tuck a piece of dryfish or salted raw meat into my mouth, or stop me with a gesture, cautioning me to listen. To her words, to the wind, to the trees and the sounds in the night.

Her stories explained my world. Later, in early grade school, a different world was explained in stories my teachers told, and in the storybooks used to teach me to read. In a few years, I heard and saw those stories repeated on every screen and every magazine cover and from every pulpit. My grandmother's stories had explained a sensible world where bears and the forest listened to my words, spiders carried lessons, and owls appeared with warnings. Everything about our person, from our fingernails to our clothing and our words, was filled with the spirit we placed there and could harm us if we failed to take care.

My grandmother's stories were inhabited by reasonable beings who could be expected to help me or harm me depending on my actions, my appearance, and especially my words. The stories from teachers and preachers and actors described a different world, the one in which I was forced to live and to travel, a world where my appearance by its nature worked against me, my actions judged by ill-fitting standards and often found unfit, and my words most often ignored or rebuked. After a while I was silenced. After a while when I spoke it was only to repeat the words I heard from the pulpit or from the professor. After a while I could no longer hear the forest, and worse, the forest could no longer hear me.

After I came home, I worked for two summers at the Naakaahidi Theater in Juneau, where I was part of an Alaska Native cast that told old stories and sang old songs. Several persons acted out a story as a narrator stood at a microphone reciting the words. Actors walked across the brightly lit stage and down the few stairs into the dimmed seating area, where a fire pit became part of the story. Another person sat at the drums. We took turns acting and speaking and beating the drum. When it was our turn to act, we placed carved wooden masks over our faces and covered ourselves with bearskins and leather, following the highly stylized movements and gestures blocked out during the month-long rehearsal. When it was our turn to narrate, we stood at the microphone and recited the provided script. Our assigned aim was to repeat word for word, pause for pause, the same phrases each time, following the movements of the actors in a choreographed production at the end of which we would all stand onstage and introduce ourselves to the audience of tourists who were thrilled simply to see real Natives and to hear us tell our stories. The two big productions were Keet Shagoon, the story of Naatsilanei, the Tsaagweidí man who first carved the Killer Whale into existence, and The Woman Who Married a Bear, an old story my grandmother had told to me those many years before.

Many cultures tell the story of the woman who married a bear, which reveals the kinship between animals and humans, and which underscores the importance of one's words. I enjoyed drumming to the story of Keet Shagoon, and I was edified to learn where killer whales came from. I took great pleasure in narrating the familiar story of The Woman Who Married a Bear. But it was when my turn came to clothe myself in the bearskin that I became something more than myself.

I walked in the manner of a bear, bending over to place my left leg deliberately forward, and then my left arm. Then my right leg solidly in its confident step, then my right arm. A few steps like this, then I raised up in a shudder, moving my hide-covered head back and forth as though smelling the air, and dropped heavily back to the floor, swaying my head and raising my shoulders into a telltale brown bear hump.

"Some people just have a brown bear inside them," the director said when we first tried out for the role, and I had to agree.

The best moment was at the end of the final scene, when the woman submits to her inner nature and covers herself in the robe in preparation for killing her brothers. The person acting the woman's part had to hold the skin in her arms and then unfold it and cast it around behind her body, encircling herself with it, making it fall on her shoulders at the moment she, and the actor playing her, turned into a bear.

Several years after I acted out the role of that woman who married a bear, I worked as a shipboard naturalist aboard Alaska state ferries, where it was my responsibility to present programs on various Alaskan topics. One favorite program was on the brown bear and black bear of Southeast Alaska, for which I was provided a black bear hide and a brown bear hide. Carrying them up to the boat deck to display during one of my programs, I was stopped by a couple of the stewards who wanted to admire the skins. I asked if they wanted to see me walk like a bear. Of course they said yes.

I handed one skin to a steward and unfolded the other, casting it around behind my body, encircling myself with it, allowing it to fall on my shoulders, placing my left leg deliberately forward, then my left arm, then my right leg solidly in its confident step, then my right arm. A few steps like this, then I raised up in a shudder, moving my hide-covered head back and forth as though smelling the air, and dropped heavily back to the floor, swaying my head and raising my shoulders in a telltale brown bear hump. The bear was still inside me.

When I was a child in the village, my mother and my grandmother fed me treats of raw hamburger, rolled into bite-sized balls and sprinkled with salt. A nibble of raw bacon was a second treat often folded into my waiting open mouth. I was made to understand hierarchy; I never questioned or challenged any of my elders. My mother and grandmother considered loyalty and endurance and silence to be part of my Wolf clan nature. To them, feeding me raw meat simply encouraged my natural temperament.

Eagles and ravens and brown bear and wolves are more than crests. They declare their own existence. The beings symbolized by these images have become elements of essential value. They are more than designs to lay on a blanket or post. They trace the design that must be placed on one's life. To typify the best traits of one's crest brings honor to the clan.

My earliest memories of my mother include her scowl. Even her widest smile always hinted at a harsh unfading frown. Throughout my life, any friends I brought to meet her were at first frightened by her fierce glare. The lines between her brows etched deeply, even in death. I had never understood why my mother at first glance seemed so belligerent. In only a few minutes her sharp humor and fearless generosity made friendly work of everyone she met, but she never treated strangers to her smile. Years after she died, I studied Lingít history and culture. In lectures and in texts, I found discussions of the clan crest on the individual's personality. Hidden in chapter notes at the back of one book, I found in an explanation of clan-owned facial expressions a reference to the Kaagwaantaan scowl. For the Wolf clan, it is a thing of value.

Behind the southeast wind, a woman's voice is wailing. I lie alone in the night, hoping to hear. Did I hear, a moment ago, a woman crying? But the sound becomes a melody, or an imagined moan, or silence. In the middle of this darkness, in the middle of the night, I comfortably renew another regret.

Among my people it is the practice to own the right to certain crests. My grandmother taught me I am Eagle, I am Wolf. Remember who you are, she always said. She reminded me that it was not by accident that the bear came to be my cousin. When I went too near the forest for berries or to play, she was sure to tell me I must speak to my cousin the bear. I must let him know that I am his relative, and he is not to harm me. I must tell him who I am.

Long ago, my grandmother said, a woman went into the woods and found herself alone there. She slipped on a pile of bear dung and spilled her berries. She cursed the bear that had made her slip and fall. But the bear heard her, and came to her as a man, and they married and had children, and those children became our cousins. That woman stayed gone from her own people for a long long time. And when the woman finally came back home, she was a stranger. She was no longer only a Wolf, only an Eagle. Now she was also a Bear. In a way, I am like that woman who married a bear. I, too, was gone for a long, long time. And when I came back I, too, was a stranger.

Years have passed since I came back home. I walk by where my dog is buried in the village near the place where my own path began. The old house was torn down long ago. I visit my mother's grave where she is buried near my grandmother. Near my great-grandmother. I know there is room there for me.

The gentle mountains embrace me, the channel is again at my feet. I hear the winter wind telling me things that only my grandfather knows. I contemplate my footprints in portions of my path, and in places alongside, I see other steps. I hear other voices. I remember other stories. I wait for my grandchildren to visit me, and when they come, I tell them stories. I teach them to sing their own songs. *Kaagwaantaan dach xan. Kaagwaantaan daxdaheen.* I tell them the words my own grandmother said to me: The spiders are your friends. The wind is your grandfather. The bear is your cousin.

Remember who you are.

Sunrise green covers the rotting trees that have fallen into the muskeg. The slime in the hidden clearing spreads itself green across the dormant pond. Along the path to this place are tomorrow's berries; today they are only buds. Pinkened green buds flawlessly mark where another day's sun will rise on a cluster of berries. One pinkened bud is sweeter than grass. On bushes of other berries, tender branches eagerly rush to a sticky end. With one glad thumbnail I nick a leaf-covered shoot and peel its spring-time skin. Inside, I find another taste of green.

A tree stump rests in the wet muskeg, covered with thick soft moss, surrounded by Hudson Bay tea and stunted pines. Low-growing bashful flowers. At the edge of the climax forest, a tall wide spruce slowly sur-renders unrobed branches from its bog side, its bark already covered with moss. It is about to fall into the muskeg.

I stand on the wooden walkway distancing myself from my compan-ions, who are there to listen to the lecture and explanations of the forester. But I've been home for only a few short years, and I am here to feel this place. I am here to smell this wet. I am here to see sparkles hanging from the needles of bristly stunted pines. I am here to be astonished at the rain-drops beading themselves into a transparent necklace and hanging from every leaf.

Here and there, berries pace themselves in the bog, shining red like drops of ruby blood. A jay darts out of the forest for a hasty look, and flies quickly back into the dim shaded safety. On every leaf on every plant on every square inch of covered ground, a wet jewel hangs ready to drop and add its dampness to the bog. In every single drop, the clouded sun-light taps its conductor's staff and readies itself for a symphony.

At sunrise, the bear awakens. She hears a familiar sound. She raises her head and blinks at the already-bright day. Beside her, the cubs stretch. They feel lazy. They've spent the winter fattening themselves on their mother's generosity, and they are not as anxious as she to leave the warm den and follow the sound of springtime into the wakening day. The bear stretches. She dares the sunlight. She looks around her.

Snow still covers much of the land, but she smells meadow plants and yellow cabbage shoots and grasses. Her mouth awakens to the memory of sedge. She will head slowly in the direction of the water. Somewhere in the unknown distance, salmon have prepared this place in their minds.

They have pictured in their minds that they will return to waters near this place. She starts off down the hill.

At the edge of a village, a child waits in her mother's womb, listening to the stories and the songs of her clan and to the music of the land. She holds within her all the life, all the promise, all the seeds of the clan. Already her mother teaches her what she will transfer to our future.

The bear's cubs follow. Not far downhill, she stops to taste an early clover. She continues down the hill. Behind her, the cubs nibble on sedge stalks. The bear makes her way to a sunlit clearing. It is dawn. She begins to eat in earnest. At the edge of an upwelling meadow, she stops. She waits. Every once in a while she dips her curious nose beneath the grass, hoping to catch the undergrowth promise of coming spring greens. She drools at the thought of early morning blossoms. The sun tells her the time is near. The grasses tell her the time is near.

It is almost time to begin.

Young Tom dragged the skiff onto the beach, unloaded his tarp and his gear, and glanced at the sky. Low clouds promised rain. Slippery rocks formed a bed where he tied the skiff at high water; at low tide it would be nestled in the stones, loosely anchored, waves barely reaching the stern, their gentle lapping keeping time to his drunken crooning, the skiff rocking in a pleasant invitational dance as Young Tom polished off the beer he held, even when drunk remembering to save most of the vodka for the morning to knock the edge off his fuzzy never-sober hangover and yesterday's resolve to make a better life.

After unpacking the boat, he found his regular campsite under the trees not far from the shoreline. He laid a tarp on the ground, shook out his old sleeping bag, gathered dry hidden branches, and built a fire. By now it was almost dark, the day fading faster, falling behind distant mountains. The sun was going home.

Young Tom opened a can of beans and another beer. He drank the beer all in one gulp, the cold wet liquid satisfying him, filling his mouth and streaming down his chin. He felt like a man. With the fire crackling reassurance, Tom sat back on a comfortable rock. He tossed his empty beer can into the bushes. He noticed flattened cans left over from other visits, some of them clearly not his brand. He'd always wondered who else came here, why he never saw anyone, where they liked to fish. He didn't think they knew his favorite spot in the middle of the inlet unmarked by any sign except the angle it made with the tall tree under which he now sat, its equal measure between the shores, the feel of its depth.

The hairs on his neck lifted. His chest flinched. He heard something move in the bushes. He was suddenly sorry he didn't own a gun anymore — he'd hawked it two years ago and now he never went hunting for deer meat unless someone took pity on him and lent him a gun and brought him along with them. When that happened, he liked to go south of Taku Inlet in the winter, killing at least one deer and fighting the ice and wind back to Juneau, hanging and butchering the meat and bragging over the hunt. He liked to make soup out of the scraps, elbowing Mabel out of the way; only he knew how to simmer it all day so it tasted like the soup Auntie Susie used to make.

But he knew the sound he'd heard was no deer. They didn't come this near the beach until after a deep snow. Tom swayed to his feet and peered into the darkened forest. Blurred shadows offered only indefinite shapes. The sound continued. An unmistakable musk reached him and caked his nostrils. He saw the bear.

At first it was no more than a large broad shadow against the backdrop of rustling bushes. It looked in his direction, its nose stroking the air. The memory of bar talk strove to break through Tom's befuddled thoughts. Bear. Xóots. My father's brother.

"Don't hurt me," he tried to say to the bear. "I'm going fishing tomorrow." Tom swayed, his balance as unsteady as his words. "You're not supposed to hurt me, brother-in-law," he reminded the bear. "I only want my own share." The bear paid attention to him, waiting for the right words. Tom struggled to stand straight. He struggled to be brave. "I only want what is meant for me."

The bear walked back into the forest. Tom didn't know how many minutes or hours passed before he forced himself to move. After a while he sat and poked the fire. He drank his last beer and took a couple nips of vodka. Twice he sensed a soundless movement but he couldn't make himself turn his head to look. There were worse things than a bear.

He covered up with the worn sleeping bag and wrapped himself in the tarp. He passed out almost at once. If in the middle of the night a woman cried in the forest, he was unable to hear her grief.

Young Tom drunkenly grasped one last clumsy time for his woozy rowboat, but it was much much farther away than he'd first supposed. His arms began waving of their own accord, his eyes sinking back in his head, unfocused, blurring, of no more use to him than that day so long ago in a Taku Wind snowstorm when a cloud of tiny icicles froze in the act of falling from his lashes and shrouded his vision so that he was forced to feel his way along the sides of the South Franklin Street buildings, recounting to himself each doorway, each window, each step: this doorway must be that old apartment where they lived that time he got candy for Patricia one afternoon when she was sick, this window must be the empty place next door where that family from somewhere in Arizona stayed until the landlord came with two lawyers and three policemen and evicted them, god, when she saw them coming, Lucille said they must have murdered someone but it turned out that they'd done something worse, they'd taken money from a property owner, this door jammed up against the sidewalk where the bump in the concrete tripped you if you weren't careful must be that high-priced little grocery store where he ran for aspirin a couple of times a week when Lucille was still drunk from the night before but didn't have any beer, hadn't yet found some man to tease or flatter or blackmail into buying today's supply so a couple of aspirin and a pack of cigarettes would do her until some stray man walked by, migod how much it felt like heartbreak those first few times he caught her dripping spit on other guys, letting them hold her around her flabby waist, flabby but she was still his woman, he'd wanted to cover her skin, pull down her sweater, force her away from drunk groping hands but he knew she'd be angry and probably wouldn't come with him, would push him away and scream and make a scene and call him names and remind him and everyone listening of all his faults, tell his few remaining secrets to the world so they'd laugh at him and talk it over and decide that having a bum for a father, one who laid in the street with piss all over his pants and slobbered in the gutter until the wagon came and took him away for a few days, cleaning him up and drying him out and feeding him soft cereal and warm bland soup until he talked them into letting him go, promising them that he was sober now for sure, he'd learned his lesson no mistake, not only would he never take another drink of beer or wine or vodka, but even more important than that, he would never never make fun of another tourist, calling them names and pointing at them and telling them that fish climb trees to lay eggs on the branches, no he'd never never never again laugh out loud at another tourist, and they'd let him go and the first thing he'd do was find a party or bum a drink or sit on a stoop until somebody anybody stopped to talk, that's all it would take for his father to start talking and keep talking until somebody anybody by god broke down and said they'd buy him a drink—all that was already bad enough without everyone knowing the rest of Young Tom's few secrets that Lucille would be glad to tell, probably did tell anyone anytime, anything for a drink, and he supposed that his friends knew about that time Lucille got horny and when no one else was around for her to seduce she tried to have sex with Young Tom but by then he was so disgusted and sickened by her that he was just a lump of indifferent flesh, and he supposed that Nadine had heard about it too, even though Young Tom was sure she'd never thought about him that way, they'd known each other since they were still babies, for god's sake they were like brother and sister, he'd always kept in his mind the image of the two of them as toddlers sitting on the floor in the early morning sunlight, catching dust motes, their pudgy sticky fingers smeared with cracker crumbs, his mother on the cot with her face turned toward the wall, Auntie Susie closing the door and leaving them to their own devices, they were family, no doubt about it, but still he didn't want her or anyone else to know his secrets, what even the thought of Lucille could do, even right up to the end, even after he divorced her and married Mabel, how just the thought of her made him cringe and hide his face and falter—what if she came back to town! After all, she'd known him when he was young, and she'd given him his only child—or at least he thought Patricia was his child, but come to think of it he couldn't really be sure, the only thing he was sure about was that Lucille slept around on him right from the beginning and never stopped sleeping around, so how could he be sure that Patricia was his daughter—he realized that when he got back to Juneau he should get one of those paternity tests, make sure what's what, he resolved that when he got back to Juneau he'd look into it, but what if Patricia wasn't his daughter, that would mean that the grandchildren weren't his either, that would make him sad but what would it do to Mabel, she loved those kids and they weren't her grandkids in any case, most likely she wouldn't care either way, she'd probably tell him not to bother, tell him he should keep loving them no matter what because what counted was love, not whether Lucille happened to get a baby from him or from some other man one drunken night, what counted was love, that was the only true and certain thing, so Young Tom promised himself that when he got back to Juneau he'd make sure everyone knew how much how much he loved his Mabel, how much he appreciated her, the way she took care of him no matter what, how faithful she'd been, how caring, how tender, how warm, how much he wished he was in her arms almost every single time he went out on the boat and found himself drunk and falling in the water and grasping one last clumsy time for his woozy rowboat, which was now even farther away from him than it had been only a moment ago, it was getting farther away every second, making Young Tom realize he had to swim, swim for the boat or for the shore, and he flailed his arms and gulped salty water, this one first time the thought piercing his brain that he might not make it, the fright of drowning the worst in his life, worse by far than any fight any fall any heartbreak, for it was common knowledge that anyone who died by drowning was in danger of rescue by land otter people, that living among the land otter people was worse than dying, and Young Tom determined in one instant that he would swim to shore, he would dry himself over a fire that would magically appear on the beach, he would be seen by all the search planes and all the boats that would rally to save him and take him back to Juneau, where he would be a hero and find a good job, one that paid good money, and he'd never go out on a boat again and he'd never take another drink and he'd be a good husband to Mabel and a good father to Patricia and even a good son to Old Tom and a good friend to everybody and he would never let another swallow of salt water fill his mouth — *migod he should never have brought that last pint of vodka or even the beer* — he couldn't feel the tears on his skin or hear his last bubbling gasps as his face sank into the cold wet hidden inlet where the smell of the ocean, the feel of the spray, the sound of the gulls, the taste of the salt, the sight of mountain behind mountain behind island behind island, falling back and back in shadows and gray and dark green would never change.

Remember that the land is enspirited. It is quickened. When as you conduct your life you chance to see an eagle, or a wolf, or a bear, remember that it too is conducting its life, and it sees you as well.

As does a tree. And the forest itself. The very land sees you.

When you remember this, and feel this, and know this, you will want to hug the land. You will want to embrace it. And when that happens, you can be sure that the land feels the same way about you.

The land loves you. She misses her children.

ACKNOWLEDGMENTS

Without Sherry Simpson, who unfailingly offered gracious encouragement, this work would have had a far more difficult beginning. Without Liz Dodd, who generously shared her valuable time and considerable talent, this work would have had a far more difficult completion. I am indebted to both.

Jeane Breinig remains a constant inspiration; Jo-Ann Mapson exemplifies steadfast integrity. These powerful women have helped me understand what it means to believe in myself.

The Juneau Arts and Humanities Council provided financial support at the closing stages of this work, for which I am sincerely grateful.

I owe my deepest thanks to Nora and Richard Dauenhauer and their work, and to those elders, relatives, and friends who have shared with me a portion of their knowledge and experiences, including Agnes Bellinger, Richard Dalton, Eugene King, Richard McKinley, Connie Paddock, Florence Sheakley, Thomas Thornton, and Rosita Worl, among many others. *Gunalchéesh.*

ABOUT THE AUTHOR

Born in Juneau, Alaska, Ernestine Hayes is a member of the Wolf House of the Kaagwaantaan clan of the Lingít. She is an assistant professor of English at the University of Alaska Southeast and is the recipient of the Explorations 2002 Alaska Native Writer's Award. She has won recognition in Native oratory and storytelling. Her writing has appeared in Travelers Tales Alaska, *The Anchorage Press*, Rasmuson Foundation grantees' stories, and the *Juneau Empire* opinion column Edge of the Village. Her current projects include a collection of linked short stories, a study of Raven tales, and a comprehensive history of the Lingít. She is the grandmother of four children.

3-9-07